William Emerson Baker

Guide to the Ridge Hill Farms, Wellesley, Mass. and Social Science

Reform

Vol. 1

William Emerson Baker

Guide to the Ridge Hill Farms, Wellesley, Mass. and Social Science Reform
Vol. 1

ISBN/EAN: 9783337297626

Printed in Europe, USA, Canada, Australia, Japan

Cover: Foto ©Lupo / pixelio.de

More available books at **www.hansebooks.com**

RIDGE HILL FARMS

WELLESLEY, MASS.

AND

OCIAL SCIENCE REFORM.

SEPTEMBER, 1877.

BOSTON:
GETCHELL BROS., PUBLISHERS AND PRINTERS,
252 WASHINGTON STREET.
1877.

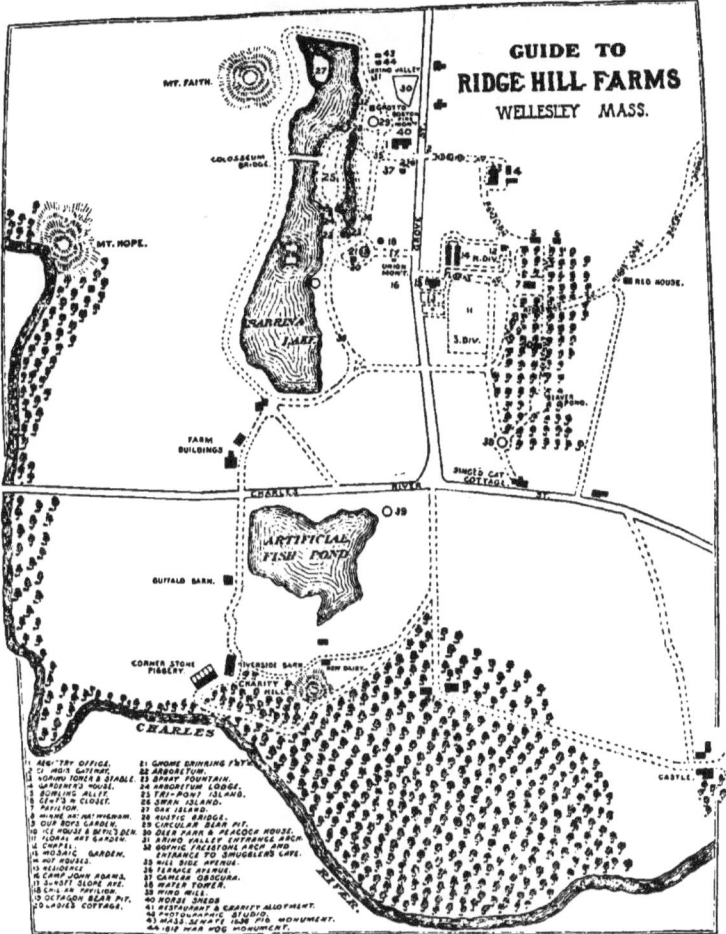

GUIDE TO
RIDGE HILL FARMS
WELLESLEY MASS.

MT. FAITH.

MT. HOPE.

COLOSSEUM BRIDGE.

FARM BUILDINGS

UNION MONT.

RED HOUSE.

N. DIV.

S. DIV.

SINGED CAT COTTAGE

ARTIFICIAL FISH POND

BUFFALO BARN.

CORNER STONE PIGGERY

RIVERSIDE BARN

CHARLES RIVER

CASTLE.

1. REGISTRY OFFICE.
2. MAIN GATEWAY.
3. ALARM TOWER & STABLE.
4. GARDENER'S HOUSE.
5. BOWLING ALLEY.
6. GENTS CLOSET.
7. PAVILION.
8. MAINE ART. MONUMENT.
9. OUR BOYS GARDEN.
10. ICE HOUSE & DEVILS DEN.
11. FLORAL ART GARDEN.
12. CHAPEL.
13. MOSAIC GARDEN.
14. HOT HOUSES.
15. RESIDENCE.
16. CAMP JOHN ADAMS.
17. SUNSET SLOPE AVE.
18. CHILEAN PAVILION.
19. OCTAGON BEAR PIT.
20. LADIES COTTAGE.
21. GNOME DRINKING FNTN.
22. ARBORETUM.
23. SPRAY FOUNTAIN.
24. ARBORETUM LODGE.
25. TRI-PONT ISLAND.
26. SWAN ISLAND.
27. OAK ISLAND.
28. RUSTIC BRIDGE.
29. CIRCULAR BEAR PIT.
30. DEER PARK & PEACOCK HOUSE.
31. ARING VALLEY ENTRANCE ARCH.
32. GOTHIC FREESTONE ARCH AND
    ENTRANCE TO SMUGGLERS CAVE.
33. HILL SIDE AVENUE.
34. TERRACE AVENUE.
35. CAMERA OBSCURA.
36. WATER TOWER.
37. WIND MILL.
38. HORSE SHEDS
39. RESTAURANT & CHARITY ALLOTMENT.
40. PHOTOGRAPHIC STUDIO.
41. MASS. SENATE 1636 PIG MONUMENT.
42. 1812 WAR HOG MONUMENT.

THE RIDGE HILL FARMS

A RE situated in Wellesley, Mass., fourteen miles from Boston by the Boston & Albany Railroad. They comprise eleven farms, owned by Wm. Emerson Baker, of Boston, who first bought, in 1868, two farms aggregating 230 acres. By subsequent purchases the estate now encloses 820 acres. On the west and south it has the Charles River for a boundary nearly four miles. About one mile northeast from the Pavilion Grove is a singularly formed Ridge over one mile in length, thickly shaded by Oak, Pine and Chestnut trees, making, with fern glens and weird nature, an unusually picturesque walk. This Ridge — the approach to which is too intricate to be found without a guide — suggested the name of the Ridge Hill Farms. But the owner has made such extensive improvements that a large area of these farms have now more of the characteristics of an Educational Park. Numerous private and quite original fêtes have been here given; some of them so extensive as to assemble three thousand guests. These have led to such publicity as to excite a wide-spread desire to visit this estate, so curiously combining art with nature — quaint history and comical amusements.

The applications from strangers for permission to visit the grounds, buildings and the Grotto, liberty to shelter carriages in the horse-sheds, and to use the row-boats, &c., have become so numerous, and when granted so expensive, that the owner, in order to get any privacy, is either compelled to destroy all his works, or else submit to the *inevitable*, and, under some system, which in any case requires much care and constant supervision, regulate the privileges granted.

These privileges have been grossly abused by the thefts of plants, fruits and exposed articles, the careless handling and breaking of valuable ornaments, ferns, and of twigs from trained trees, strewing the grounds and ponds with paper and refuse from the luncheon basket, feeding the pet animals with tobacco, &c. Very many visitors, who carefully conform to the proprieties of life while at their homes, have here proved, in numerous selfish ways, their thoughtless disregard of the expense caused to the proprietor. This reckless want of consideration for the courtesies extended to them provokes the closing of the gates to all.

But in order to avoid this, — to gratify the well-disposed, who hesitate to ask favors, to control the indiscreet, who are the most numerous solicitants, and save himself and household numerous applications from strangers, — the owner has granted concessions as follows : —

All applicants to visit this estate, approved at 13 *West Street, Boston,* or at the *Registry Office* at the Farms, where *every one is required* to register his or her name, will be allowed *free access* to the grounds and the pet animals on the visiting days,

Wednesdays and Saturdays.

But no visitors will be permitted to enter the Grotto, nor the Norino Tower, the Camera or other buildings, except upon payment of the small *service fee* (10 cents), necessary to pay the one-half cent to each of the twenty attendants there required, both as guides and to prevent the thefts and other indiscretions which have been so frequent and annoying. This regulation avoids all necessity of gifts to employés, and is objectionable only to that class who prefer to live at others' expense.

In order to deter visitors coming on other than the regular visiting days, a charge of twenty-five cents, for service-fee coupons, will be made on other than Wednesdays and Saturdays. *Thursdays will be most liable to be reserved exclusively for the guests of the owner.*

For this *service fee* visitors will receive three coupons, one of which will be given up upon admission to each of the following places: Norino Tower, including Arcadium for Little Folks and the Tivoli Hall — the Round Tower, Smugglers' Cave, Stalactite Grotto — and the Camera.

Upon showing any one of these coupons admission will also be had, *when the convenience of the owner will permit*, to the carriage-house and stable departments, to the Chapel, the Bowling Alley, the Pavilion Hall, the Conservatory part of the Hot-Houses, and the Boat-House.

Should the service fees aggregate more than the expenditures specially arising from the admission of visitors, such surplus will be given to the Charity Fund.

On arriving at the estate, the Registry Office will be found on the west side of Grove Street. Here every visitor is *required* to register his or her name.

𝔗𝔬 𝔱𝔥𝔢 𝔘𝔭𝔭𝔢𝔯 𝔊𝔯𝔬𝔲𝔫𝔡𝔰 𝔈𝔞𝔰𝔱 𝔬𝔣 𝔊𝔯𝔬𝔳𝔢 𝔖𝔱𝔯𝔢𝔢𝔱.

Enter by the CHAMOIS GATEWAY, opposite the Registry Office, so named from the *chamois* on the granite piers.*

The *Conservatory Lawn* on your right was an apple orchard in 1873.

The *Portulacca* bed bordering this lawn and Grove Street is seven hundred feet in length.

The roof of the stable is decorated by a large allegorical painting of the "*Horen*" leading forth the Horses of the Sun, — by John Gibson, R.A.

---

* Strangers entering the grounds by any other than the Chamois Gateway will be regarded as trespassers. Carriages will not be admitted.

The Horen were known as the attendants of the Gods (particularly of Aphrodite), — as Guardians to the Gates of Heaven, — Goddesses of the Seasons, — of the *Hours* of the day, and also of Eternal Youth.

The colored circular cartoon on the west side, representing the controlling effect of music on animals, is from the mythological fable of Orpheus, by Engerth, in Vienna.

The oil cartoon below it pictures the German mythological legend of the Walküren, the handmaids of Wotan (Jupiter), whose duties were to select the warriors slain in battle and conduct them to Walhalla (the eternal home of the brave). These Walküren and their wild horses were supposed to be immortal. The frame of this stable was moved one thousand feet, placed on its present site, and reconstructed in 1872. The tower adjoining was erected in 1874, for a reservoir tank. But a more extended water service was devised before the tower was finished. The proximity of the tower and stable gave the architectural appearance of a church. In order to destroy this illusion, the owner had the entire outside of the stable painted black, the trimmings bronze green, and relieved this by covering the fluting and dentals with gold leaf. The striking effect of this bold departure, defiantly controls the mind, as intended.

Enter NORINO TOWER (from the word *Norino*, Greek, meaning to make known, to point out, gain knowledge of).

The 1st department, twenty feet in height, is marked *"Architecture in Construction and in Dress."* Here are found photographs of famous buildings, models of the Alhambra, steel and chain armors of past centuries, pictures, chromos, raised figures on rice paper, and statues of bronze, clay and papier maché, showing the costumes of various centuries.

Ascend the *Donkey Stairway*, so named from the appropriate paintings on the side wall, to the

2d floor, marked " *Chemical, Mechanical* and *Electrical*," which is devoted to apparatus, models, &c., explanatory of these subjects.

3d floor: "SANITARY. *Suggestive of mental amusement and less materia medica.*"

4th floor: " *Optics, illusions and delusions.*" Here are twelve round windows of varied colored glass, showing the outside nature as in the four seasons of spring, summer, autumn and winter; also other peculiar sunlight reflections.

5th floor: " *Harmony in outlines and colors, as well as in vibrative brass or human tongues.*" Art is here exhibited in toned colors by flowers, by stuffed birds and chromos on musical subjects, and here also is a curious reed music box and the stringed instrument called the Zither.

6th floor: "*The End of Life. What is it? What the aim of life? What the record at the end?*" Here are found engravings of Martin's wonderfully elaborate paintings of the Pandemonium, Fall of Babylon, Satan in Council; also The Crucifixion, Canova's Tomb, La Mort, allegorical souvenir of the French Revolution of 1848, and a large engraving, 200 years old, allegorical of the Day of Judgment, by Senonien.

Twenty-two feet above this floor, we reach the 7th department, or roof, marked " *What we see about us. Looking down on our peculiar world; looking up to the clear yet dark beyond.*"

Descend to the second floor, and by the *Doggerel Gallery* (the side-walls of which are covered with paintings, casts, &c., of dogs), pass to the ARCADIUM FOR LITTLE FOLKS, which hall, thirty by fifty feet, is filled with oddities both to amuse and to instruct children, consisting of mechanical toys, music boxes, dolls, baby houses, puzzles, pictures, skating rink, and an endless variety of other automatic attractions, educating the child student by suggesting the *reason why.* The table spread with cold lunch, the Japanese curiosities and other novelties, induce adults as well as children to linger here. Descend thence to the

TIVOLI HALL, which is also thirty by fifty feet: here
are found Billiard Table, Erratic Spinner, Tivoli, and many
other table games for adults, a very peculiar mechanical
piano, curious views of Paris on glass inlaid with pearl,
porcelain *hautes reliefs* of the Erl King, Mephistopheles
and Faust, of War and Peace, art engravings of Raphael's
Twelve Hours, natural leaves from trees perforated in
portraits and scenery, &c.

Passing through the communicating door to the First
Department of Norino Tower, and out at the same door
by which you entered the Tower, proceed to the south side
of the *Stable*, on which are found several colored cartoons
having comical reference to draught animals.

At the further or north end of the Carriage Department
will be found the old-fashioned coach once owned by
Governor Eustis, and in which his guest, General Lafayette, rode when he was received by the city of Boston,
with a grand ovation, in the year 1825.

If admitted to the Stable, take notice of the peculiar
arrangement of the stalls permitting the horses to see the
visitors without turning round, and thus avoid being
frightened.

The hopper of the automatic feed-box being filled and
the indicator of the clock set, the trap will fall and the
feed pass to the horses at the hour indicated, thus soon in-

ducing the horses to watch all clocks, thoughtful of the ﬁcu hour.

Leaving the Stable, proceed by the Norino Avenue to the Album Bowling Alley in Pavilion Grove, which is so named because the owner makes use of its side-walls and ceiling, as others use a scrap-book, — for his private collection of newspaper and other scraps, and also souvenirs pertaining to his eventful life. This is generally closed to all but guests of the Proprietor. If permitted to enter it, the visitor can here pass a half-hour very acceptably in examining the peculiar illustrations, original programmes and other souvenirs of the many fêtes given at Ridge Hill Farms. On the roof of this Album Bowling Alley there is a chime of bells moulded from a new kind of bronze for the Boston Peace Jubilee Coliseum.

The greater part of the gifts received at the " *Tinth* " anniversary of the Marriage Fête were lost by the fire on October 28, 1876; but a very quaint collection of these tin gifts saved from the fire is here collected, consisting of Bells, Slippers, Decanters, Jewelry, Hats, Graters, &c.*

The "UNION CHAPEL" has marked over the entrance, "Creed, *Liberty of Conscience, Faith, Hope and Charity*." From its ceiling are suspended Doves, Birds, &c.; on

---

* Gents' Toilette at the east end of the Bowling Alley.

its walls are appropriate photographs; and the following
mottoes in blue and gold are over the windows : —

"Count that day lost whose low descending sun
    Views from thy hand no worthy action done."

"*Do* noble things, not dream them all day long,
    And so make life, death, and that vast forever
One grand, sweet song."

"Look not mournfully into the past —
    The *present* is yours :
    Go forth into the future with courage
    And a manly heart."

"Duty be thy Polar Guide, —
    Do the right what e'er betide :
    Haste not, rest not; conflicts past,
    God shall crown your work at last."

There is no one so bad but has
    Some good in him.
There is no one so good who
    Cannot be better.

"In things essential, UNITY;

In non-essentials, LIBERTY;

In all things, CHARITY."

This Chapel was dedicated at a social fête on the 4th of July, 1869, one year after the purchase of the first farm.

The PAVILION HALL in the Grove was erected in 1875, but an addition was made for the *Liberty of Conscience Fête,* given to the ministers of all the differing denominations, September 20, 1876. It is 30 x 140 feet, with two side-rooms and Orchestre Gallery in an L on the south side. This Pavilion Hall is used for private fêtes and banquets. It is generally closed to visitors. But blow the call-whistle at the north front door, and the attendant in adjacent rear building will respond if admission be granted.

The Log Cabin east of this Pavilion is used as its kitchen.

In the PAVILION GROVE will be found the LEAKY BOOT DRINKING FOUNTAIN, from Berlin, and several ornamental enclosures, and pet animal houses for coons, squirrels and turtle doves.

One of these is made of piping, for the two raccoons, *Mr.* and *Mrs. Davy Crockett.* and the *twin-baby Crockett-Coons.*

One large cage, cone-shaped, is for the black Florida fox squirrel, called *Nut-ty Black,* and the two gray squirrels

called the *Gray Nun-such Sisters*, although they so quar-
rel for tidbits as to prove a lack of *charity* for each other.

Another large cage, cone-shaped, encloses the *Ring-neck
Doves* and *Love Birds*. These are well symbolical of
Horatio Harris, who died in Roxbury, in 1875, from whose
estate this cage came, and of whom it may be written:
He was exceptionally faithful and charitable, and acutely
sensitive of any publicity of his charity.

Reader, what is *your* aim in life, and what will be *your*
record at the end?

The other four cages, which are found during fine
weather east of the Chapel in the Pavilion Grove, contain
two sulphur-crested cockatoos from South America, known
as *Mr.* and *Mrs. Sulphuretta Cockatooto.*

One rose-colored cockatoo, called *Rose Chatterbox.*

One blue and red macaw from Mexico, named *Anti-
blue-law Swearing Jack*, because he *improperly* interprets
the "Liberty of Conscience," creed of the Union Chapel
near by, and two green parrots from South America; the
one with the golden head being called *Baby Mimic*,
because she cries·like an infant, and the other called
Sister Green.

Near that for the African porcupine will be found the
Diorama, enclosed by wire walls to prevent more than
three persons examining it at the same time.

In the Grove south from Pavilion Hall, is to be erected the house for the monkeys, parrots, macaws, cockatoos, Madagascar and Bombay cats, &c., which are temporarily found in that part of the old Hot-house saved from the fire of October 28, 1876. This fire destroyed the Bell Tower, the Porcelain Building, two hot-houses and many valuable plants.

As the flames spread towards the south end of the hot-houses, the heat and smoke caused the monkeys so to chatter and screech as to bring the aid of those attempting to stay the flames. Many of the smaller monkeys were removed to the nearest convenient quarters, which happened to be the ice-house, and there allowed to cool off.

The African porcupine, *Bristling Porcus* (with one of whose quills we now do write), spread himself in such a touch-me-if-you-dare fashion that those who came to help save his life were afraid of their own lives, and therefore allowed him and the older monkeys to stay where they were; but, fortunately, the fire was put out before it destroyed the house they occupied.

The smallest monkey in the collection is named *Silly.* She is now an invalid, and weak physically as well as mentally.

The drab ring-tail monkey hangs by his tail, is gentle,

observant, and will pick your pocket so amiably that you are willing to let him do it again. He is from Brazil, and is called *Dom Pedro.*

The dark, medium-sized monkey is called *Jerry.* He is very quick, and delights in stealing feathers from the hats of lady visitors, or sampling their dress trimmings. He will forcibly exhibit his dislike of such as do not dress to suit him, by jumping against the wire netting as if he wished to tear to tatters the offending dress.

The large gray male monkey is called *Napoleon.* He has *Bridget,* the red-faced washerwoman monkey, for his wife, and in their cage should be, but seldom is, found *Bridget's* baby, the monkey *Prince Imperial.*

The lady-like gray monkey, *Emperess Josephine,* discarded wife of the gray *Napoleon,* is in the cage with *Crapo,* the most dignified of all the monkeys. This *Crapo,* quiet yet quick as lightning, has many times jumped through the open door and escaped as the custodian came to feed him.

On one occasion, as the coolness of night came on, he returned within a mile of his home, and climbed into an open window, and alarmed the inmates of the house, who were awakened by the noise apparently of burglars in the " spare chamber." When the householder opened the chamber door to investigate the noise, *Crapo* was not the only one frightened, and the door was quickly closed and locked, and *Crapo* occupied "the guest chamber" until daylight, when he left by the open window, glad to return to his home. On another escapade he visited a school-house about one mile from home, and entered the room occupied by forty boy and girl pupils. The teacher told her pupils to attend to their studies and not notice the monkey, and possibly he would ·leave. ·But *Crapo*, in one of those animal freaks which either "just happen" or are caused by animal reason, sprang for the teacher's desk, which she quickly yielded and rushed for the open door, followed by her little flock. *Crapo*, deserted, and slighted in his first attempt at teaching, joined the outside crowd of pupils. One of the larger boys picked up a stick with which to protect himself; *Crapo*, noticing this, made grimaces at the offender, jumped and caught him, tore away his jacket in three pieces, and made off with the stick.

The impressive studies this day, in animated nature, will doubtless be rehearsed by these pupils to their children and grandchildren, with as much interest as the story of Mary's little lamb at school. This old red school-house has recently been purchased, and now makes part of the Ridge Hill Farms.

Bipeds wishing to practise gymnastics, or other elevated

studies, must make early application for admission to *Cra-po's School.*

The red foxes in the goat enclosure are called *Winnie Red* and *Reddy Winner.*

The names of the goats are *Nannie-white Goatee* and *Charley-black Goatee.*

The numerous dogs on the estate, at night will come when least expected, and offer their services without being called by any name.

The carrier pigeons, making their home on the carriage-house near the Registry Office, are of the dragon species, and of direct descent from those employed at the siege of Paris. Trustingly they will come to your feet to receive a crumb of comfort, as those fed by order of the authorities of the city of Venice. They are called *Carrie Nota, Gettie Nota, Papa, Mamma, Sister* and *Brother Nota.*

The swans are named *Mr.* and *Mrs. Swan-nie Black, Mr.* and *Mrs. Swan-nie White,* and *Miss White-head.*

The names of the black bears in the Circular Bear-Pit are as follows: *Old Lady Brown, Black Nero,* young, active, treacherous; *Sitting Bull,* because he has a fancy for sitting on his haunches; and *Big Black Bruiser.*

The Madagascar cat in the monkey-cage, grunts like the pig, has wool like the llama, tail like a cat, and has feet and springs like a monkey. The Bombay cat is quiet, but the monkeys sadly repent playing with Black Bomba's tail, as they play with *Madagascar Charlie*.

Polly Gray, the African parrot in the Hot-house, will impress you with the statement that she is a "pretty Polly."

Another curious occupant of this old Hot-house is the *Diamond Beetle*, from Mexico, which, upon being sprinkled with water, will (in the dark) illumine a large room by its phophorescent eyes, which shine like emeralds of the finest quality. This beetle lives on fruits, and a procession of them in a dark night would outshine any torchlight festival that mortals ever got up. Some Spanish ladies dress their hair with these living phosphorescent beetles, confined in lace nets, which dazzle in emerald brilliancy any diamonds or other expensive jewels ever found.

In the Octagon Bear-Pit will be found, in the month of September, if life be spared, two Seneca bear cubs, now on their way north. They were captured in April, when only a few days old, by Lucius Carrier, a native of Connecticut, on Cow Creek, Indian River, Brevard County, Florida. Since the purchase of these cubs, August 11, by the proprietor of Ridge Hill Farms, the writer has made diligent search, but can find no description of these bears in any of the numerous books on Natural History.

Though differing from, they come the nearest under the head of the *Spectacled* bear, which inhabits the great mountain range extending through the whole of the South American Continent, and which are specified very briefly by Arnold and Samuels as having been largely known as the most beautiful of all bears, but of whose habits nothing has been recorded by naturalists. An extended interview with Mr. Carrier elicited the following interesting facts : The Seneca bears are well known in Brevard County, Florida. Their fur is smooth, and the dress hair-coat, light mouse color, which is hidden, as they mature in age, by a coarser growth of a darker shade. There is an iron-gray shade from the nostril back to the eyes. The eyes are smaller than those of other bears, and do not show any order of excitement under which the animal may be laboring. Fear or annoyance is first indicated by the throwing back of the ears, which are larger, wider spread and more erect than those of other bears. The female is always so peculiarly marked that it seems impossible for these bears to have existed in this or any age without some poetical legend describing the white fur only found at the breast, and there in the shape of a perfect heart.*

* Wanted for exposition in the Flirtation Tunnel, a perfect heart, not only in shape, but in *action*.

Will not Longfellow, Holmes and Whittier join hands and give us a triplet poem concerning the wonders of the fairy-land in Brevard County, Florida?

Within the confines of this range of ridges can be found the ivory-bill woodpecker, described by Audubon, the existence of which has been doubted by some ornithologists. And a profusion of the modest and of the gorgeous flowers, from the brilliant variegated grasses and their blooms, up to the royal palm, found only in Florida, the penalty, by special act of Congress, for destroying any one of which is *twenty* years' imprisonment.

Here also is found a calcareous deposit — millions of shells — known as koqueno, which are connected together by the action of the elements, in the form of ridges and caverns, great boulders of which, weighing two hundred tons, are undermined by the tides and washed away.

Tropical fruits are no less profuse, rich and varied. Its fauna are varied and beautiful, from the black and gold grasshopper, the owl which catches the food, while the gopher stands on the watch, and the snake defends their *triune* home, up to the mocking-bird, brilliant-feathered songster, and these Seneca, the most wonderful of all the bear family, which are next of kin to the *porcus* family, acknowledged as intuitively the most susceptible of education. Possibly these bears are very properly named as in direct descent from the old sage Seneca. Did *he* ever visit Flori-da? which in its profusion of beauties must differ from that of every other spot on this terrestrial sphere, and *most* resemble that of the old Garden of Eden. Will not the Mayor of Boston, and all the other city officials, Council and Aldermen, who voted to run ferry-boats to and from East Boston free to all the world, in order to increase the passenger travel to Europe by the Cunard steamships, and value of the wharf property of Noddle-Islanders, and save them (the owners) two cents ferriage when they come to the city proper to make money from those who pay nine tenths of the taxes, — will not, we repeat, these *peculiar* officials give all other Bostonians a free excursion trip to Brevard County, Florida, and charge it to the *Public Health* Department? Please engross such an act of sanitary duty (?) at once, and not refer our petition to those who may occupy your official seats after the next election. We want to dig for the old pottery, which, to the depth of fifteen feet or more, is abundant in Brevard County. We want to examine the great earth-mounds having a full-form skeleton of one who must have been from seven to nine feet in height, surrounded in a circle by an immense number of human skeleton arms, legs and bodies, lopped apart. We wish to know if we can regard the St. John, the Indian, or the Oclawaha Rivers as once the Euphrates, and this region as the apple-orchard of Adam and Eve. We wish to sit at night by the *Life-Saving Station*, told us as on the narrow neck of land between the Indian River and the Atlantic, and watch these Seneca bears who come to the sea-shore about the 20th of May, and tramp, tramp, tramp up and down the miles of beach until September 1, living upon crabs, the eggs of loggerhead turtles, and removing the corks from and drinking the contents of such bottles (said to be numerous) as float ashore, thrown overboard from the steamships going south, which vessels, to avoid steering against the northern tide of the Gulf Stream, get shoreward into the counter-current flowing south. We wish to follow the bear tracks as the human species, and the deer, coon, and other animals do to the fresh-water pools, which these bruins know best where to find, and how deep to dig : six inches sometimes will be fresh water, and twelve inches salt water. If we cannot go, please send our poets, and let them weave us a yarn concerning these wonderful beauties, and we will read it while contemplating the Seneca bears *Adam* and *Eve*, in the Octo-gon Bear-Pit at Ridge Hill Farms.

The Seneca bears when fully grown will vary in weight from 600 to 1200 pounds. If wounded, they will apply dirt to the part lacerated. Their bump of caution is prominent, they mistrust every one. They are slow but sure in their movements. While pursuing investigations concerning Seneca bears, the writer accidentally met with a taxidermist from Nova Scotia, who states that one of these Seneca bears, as herein described, with the white hair outline of a heart, was shot 200 miles from St. John, and sent to him to be taxidermisted, a few months since. The animal has never before been seen or heard of in Canada, and consequently was regarded with great wonder. As these Senecas are from the warm or equatorial regions, how did he get as far north? Can it be that there is some outlet in Nova Scotia from the *Simms* hole, which is said to run from the north pole through the subterranean fires, to the south pole? Leaving you to decide this matter, we leave this harping on the bear family, with the advice to such ladies as wish to hunt, capture or destroy him, to strike their snout, and, in the expressive language of a Pacific-coast hunter we have just interviewed, " rip open their stomach with a jack-knife." If you wish to get away, never *ascend*, but always *descend*, a hill, as the bears never descend a tree or precipice head downward, and always run down a hill in a ziz-zag course. They are so sensitive at the diaphragm as to be partially paralyzed if they descend a tree or precipice head first. When they fight, they prefer to stand erect on their hind feet. But their

most effective mode is while on their backs, so they can
scratch, hug and tear with their hind feet.

On this 21st of August, another and beautiful specimen óf
the Parrot species has been added to the collection at Ridge
Hill Farms. It is of the semi-cockatoo order — gray body
plumage, rose feathers encircling the neck, and a salmon
shade the crest. This brilliant bird was caught by B. F.
Curtis, at Hough's Neck Promontory, skirting Quincy Bay,
on land belonging to John Quincy Adams. It was contending against an attack of twelve king-birds, assisted by
several blackbirds, who evidently recognized him as a gay-
looking foreigner not yet naturalized, whom they were attempting to subjugate when rescued by Samaritan Curtis.
The town of Quincy made curiosity calls to see the rescued, but no one claimed him as his pet, and he was
regarded, by reason of his wild ways, as having escaped
from the ship which emigrated him from his African home.
He evidently had heard of the national-executive Adams
family, and though of African birth, yet believed that
his gray uniform would win him protection from the
preying blackbirds who were sorely oppressing him. This
bird speaks only in an unknown tongue — niggerish-gib-
berish. As he will probably soon speak for himself in the
American naturalized tongue, calling himself a " pretty
Polly," he has been already named after the great Roman

orator, *Roscius,* to which pre-nom the family name of Quincy is added to appropriately designate all his descendants as originating from this imported African, who placed himself under the protectorate of the American Statesmen Adams, whose acts and domain at once spot them as worthy descendants of Adam's and Eve's Garden of Eden.

Near the Pavilion Hall are also found *Mushroom Seats* from the French Department, Centennial Exhibition. The best effect of any seats on the ground is had from those placed near the junction of Pavilion Grove and Ridgeway Avenue opposite Minnehaha's Wigwam.

In this Sweet-Water Wigwam will be found a series of eight paintings portraying the evils of Intemperance, and also two stereoscopic pictures of Minnehaha, to change which, press the two buttons on each side of the box in which they are found.

Leaving this Wigwam, we reach OUR BOYS' GARDEN. The Play-House and store here found is for the sale of souvenir quills or feathers from the porcupine, peacocks, parrots, swans, &c., at Ridge Hill Farms, and to teach the children, by practical lessons in the first principles of business, value of money, keeping accounts, &c. One tenth of the proceeds to be devoted to such charity as they shall designate.

Here will also be found all that remains of the DEVIL's

DEN. This was constructed of one thousand old railroad sleepers, for the Re-Union Good-Cheer Fête given June 19, 1875. It was so called because five attendants dressed as devils — aptly representing their employment — here served claret punch to three thousand guests from the Southern States, visiting Boston to participate at the Bunker Hill Centennial. During the past winter an ice-house has been built in this *Devil's Den.*

Near the enclosure for the foxes and goat teams will be found a curious specimen plant known as the *Demonified Cereus*, from Simms' Hole near the Equator. During warm and pleasant weather this plant blossoms four or five times in each hour, which almost instantly close or fall to the ground.

The NORTH DIVISION of the *Floral Art Garden* — that between the Chapel and Hot-houses — was a vegetable garden in the early spring of 1875.

The SOUTH DIVISION, with the balustrade bordering on Pavilion Grove, was covered with pear trees and small fruit plants in January of the present year; since which time all of them have been moved, and the walks, grass-plots and floral beds made.

The three ARCHES at the south or trellis part of this *Floral Art Garden* are from the Italian Department, Centennial Exhibition.

South Garden.

The visitor's attention will be attracted on *Floral Avenue* by the chain border of foliage plants, consisting of *pyre-thrum aureum, alternanthera spathulata* and *echeveria secunda glauca*, relieved by gravels of various colors, and by the festooning of verbenas in variety on the opposite side.

The Conservatory part of the new Hot-houses, that crowned by the cupola and agave plant, is entered from the north side. That part of the Hot-houses devoted to raising fruits is not open to visitors. During the latter part of the season of 1876 some inconsiderate vandal climbed in at the window and took therefrom every one of the ripe peaches from three specimen trees. Of this order of intruders of the present season was Bridget, the gray monkey, who broke the glass and cut her hand, yet not so seriously as to say-she-ate her appetite until she had finished a large cluster of Hamburg grapes.

The *Mosaic Garden* is on the south side of the unpre-tending summer home of the owner of the estate. Here are found plats of *echeveria* and other plants arranged in unique designs to harmonize with a mosaic made of bits of white porcelain, black coal, red brick and blue glass. The Claude Lorraine mirrors revolve so as to reflect the picturesque of the Mosaic and Art Gardens.

In the Mosaic Garden will be found the *Danaïdian*

Fountain, the statue of a female figure with an urn, flowing water into the *Amymone Basin.* It is named from the mythological legend of Danaüs, son of Belus, who was King of Libya about the year B.C. 1580. He had fifty daughters, known as "The Danaïdes." His brother Ægyptus (Rameses), King of Arabia, and, by conquest, of Egypt, had fifty sons, who plotted to destroy their uncle and get his kingdom. Aided by the goddess Minerva, Danaüs built a fifty-oared vessel and fled with his daughters to Argos (Greece), and became its king. This country of Argos was extremely deficient in pure and wholesome water. Danaüs set forth with his daughters in quest of some. While Amymone, one of the daughters, was engaged in the search, she was rescued by Neptune from the intended violence of a satyr, and the god revealed to her a fountain, since called after her name. These springs are Lake Lerna, where Hercules killed the nine-headed hydra, and which fed the waters of the Danube. The sons of Ægyptus came to Argolis and entreated their uncle to bury past enmity in oblivion and to give them their cousins in marriage. Danaüs, distrustful of their promises, apparently consented, and the Danaïdes were divided among them by lot. But on the wedding day Danaüs armed the hands of the brides with daggers, and enjoined upon them to slay, in the night, their unsuspecting bridegrooms. All but Hypermnertra obeyed, and the heads of their husbands were thrown into Lake Lerna. At the command of Jupiter, Mercury and Minerva purified them from the guilt of their deed. Danaüs proclaimed gymnastic games in which the victors were to receive his forty-nine remaining daughters as prizes. Samuel Weller had probably read the doings of these forty-nine widows, which led him to caution his son against *all* " vidders."

It is said, however, that the crime of the Danaïdes did not pass without due punishment in Hades, where they were condemned to draw water forever with perforated vessels. Thus the statue of a female, bent as if by continued work, placed in the Amymone Basin, Mosaic Garden, at Ridge Hill Farms, is intended to memorialize the mythology of ancient time — 1600 B.C. — the urn, held by the female figure, through which passes the overflow water from the Water Tower, symbolizing the perforated vessels used by the Danaïdes in their eternal work.

The basins, fountains, buildings, &c., of these *Upper Grounds* have a high-service water supply from the WATER TOWER, one hundred feet high, surmounted by the statue of Neptune, eleven feet high, seen in the distance south of the PAVILION GROVE. This tower is built of red brick, with six arches, in form of a Grecian temple. The capacity of the tank is 50,000 gallons.

This reservoir is filled with water by the large *Eclipse Windmill*, thirty feet diameter, on the ornamental Wood Tower, ninety feet high. This Windmill Tower is located on the Charity Reservation (350 acres).

The aggregate length of the main and branch pipes (which are of wood and from one to six inches in diameter) connecting the Windmill and Water Tower, fountains, buildings, animal enclosures and to the overflow in Sabrina Lake, is over five miles.

West Side of Grove Street.

The Camp John Adams, for the Southern Guests at the seven-day Fraternal Welcome Fête commencing July 8, 1876, was on the Sunset Slope, west of the Mosaic Garden and of Grove Street.

Here will be found a cannon which was bought in Liverpool by English sympathizers with the South in 1861. It was run through the blockade, used by the Confederates, captured by the United States forces, recaptured by the South, and, while in use, a shell from the Northern forces struck it in the muzzle, lodged there, and disabled it.

In recognition of the social re-union hospitalities in Wellesley, in June, 1875, and in Charleston, S.C., in January, 1876, this cannon was presented to the host in Wellesley, and led to the following correspondence : —

BOSTON, June 3, 1876.
R. C. GILCHRIST,

  Commander Washington Light Infantry,

                        Charleston, S.C.

Dear Sir, — Your kind favor of May 29th is this evening received, informing me that, by Resolutions of the Washington Light Infantry of Charleston, S.C., you forward to me a Blakely (Gun), rifled, used by the Confederate army in the "late unpleasantness," and disabled by a cannon-ball striking it in the muzzle and lodging there.

This Cannon has reached me, and I shall highly value this muzzled war-fiend which you now so *kindly* level at me. I shall plant it at my Ridge Hill Farms in Wellesley, where I invite you, who stood behind it, to meet those who stood before it and shake hands *over* it. Will you not come, with your command, immediately on leaving the Philadelphia Centennial, or at some other time this summer, and accept a farmer's commissariat for one week at my Wellesley home? I shall be pleased to receive, also informally, and entertain in like fashion, as many of those ladies accompanying the members of your command to Philadelphia as can be persuaded to accept of farm-house accommodations which I will specially allot to them.

Awaiting your response, and thanking you for your Big-Gun remembrance,   I am at your service,

                           WM. E. BAKER.

HEADQUARTERS W. L. I., CHARLESTON, S.C.,

June 9, 1876.

COL. WILLIAM E. BAKER, *Tremont St., Boston.*

Colonel, — Your hospitable invitation to the Washington Light Infantry to visit the Ridge Hill Farms in Wellesley immediately on leaving Philadelphia, to accept a farmer's commissariat one week at your Wellesley home, was presented at a meeting of the company last evening; and I am instructed to inform you of their grateful appreciation of your kindness, and that as many of the command as can spare the time will be happy to accept your invitation. We hope, also, that several of our ladies will accompany us.

Truly and respectfully yours,

R. C. GILCHRIST,

Capt. Comd'g W. L. I.

Upon this acceptance of the invitation extended to the Washington Light Infantry, invitations were extended to the Clinch Rifles of Augusta Ga., the Fayetteville Independent Light Infantry of North Carolina, the officers of the Richmond Commandery Knight Templars No. 2 of Virginia, the Norfolk Light Artillery Blues of Virginia, the officers of the Washington Light Infantry of Washington, D. C., the officers of the Fifth Regiment Maryland

National Guard of Baltimore, Md., and the officers of the
" Old Guard " of New York city, with such ladies as could
be persuaded to accompany them, to encamp for one week
as guests at Ridge Hill Farms. Representative delega-
tions of these organizations accepted the invitation : — so
that the aggregate number of guests entertained for the
week was about two hundred and fifty, and on the 7th or
Charity Day, three thousand.

A general committee of fifty, including the Governor
and Ex-Governor of the State, the Mayor and President of
the Board of Aldermen of Boston, the General commanding the Forts in New England, Collector of the Port,
President of the Board of Trade, and other prominent citizens, co-operated with the host in extending a welcome to
the Southern guests, who arrived in Boston, July 8, 1876,
and received a perfect ovation from the populace while
being escorted to breakfast in Faneuil Hall, where they
were welcomed by speeches from the Governor, A. H.
Rice, the Mayor of Boston, and others.

On their reaching Ridge Hill Farms the host very informally received his guests on Conservatory Lawn, and
expressed the hope that they would immediately make
themselves AT HOME. Quarters were assigned the military
in the CAMP JOHN ADAMS, which was formed in a hollow
square, — composed of 137 wall tents and several pavilion

marquees — laid out into streets, designated by the flags
and names of the different visiting organizations. Wood
pipes were specially laid in these streets, supplied with
water from the Tank Tower, two thirds of a mile away.
The lady and civilian guests were lodged in the Virginia
Lodge, the Singed-Cat Cottage, and various other houses
on the estate. A full description of the fun, frolic and
excursions at the seven-day FRATERNAL WELCOME FETE
will be published in " *The Fêtes at Ridge Hill Farms*,"
illustrated, subscriptions for which will be received at the
Registry Office in aid of the fund to establish the Boston
Food Dispensary.

Tower Grounds.

Entering Sunset Slope, on the left is the platform that
served as the headquarters of the CAMP JOHN ADAMS.

This platform is now in process of being so covered with
a structure of wood and metal as to be permanent, and
will be painted to resemble an Army Headquarters Marquee.

This is to be the UNION MONUMENT to commemorate
the United North and South. The conception of the proprietor of the estate is as follows: The four-sided roof
will be bristling with one. thousand bayonets used in the

late strife between the North and the South. On the apex
of the cone of bayonets will be placed a white dove holding in its beak a sprig of olive-leaves. At the side entrance will be a soldier guard; one with a blue and the
other with a gray uniform. Inside is to be placed, when
finished by the artist, a large oil-painting representing a
volunteer soldier uniformed in the United States service
blue, clasping with his left hand the right hand of his affianced, a " Southern belle " (daughter of an active partici-
pant in the Southern cause, born in South Carolina),
while the soldier represented by the Confederate gray
uniform grasps with his left hand the right hand of his
affianced, a " Northern belle " (daughter of a prominent
General in the Northern forces, born in Massachusetts).
Each of these two representative soldiers from the North
and the South holds in the right hand a drawn sword,
both of which are raised and crossed over the heads of, as
if swearing protection to, their affianced.

The shadowy face and form of General Robert E. Lee is
to be seen on one side of this quartette group as if crown-
ing approval of the union of hearts and union of hopes,
while that of General U. S. Grant is similarly represented
on the other side.

Prominent in view will be seen the creed — " Liberty of
Conscience, " " Faith, Hope and Charity."

When this Union Monument is finished, there is to be placed in it a sketch (which, until the headquarters are completed, will remain in the boat-house) hastily painted in one day; copied from a small photograph of a figure moulded life-size by a sculptor in Christiana, to form one part of the group he has submitted as his design for a monument to be erected in Boston, by the Committee of Bostonians who have the matter in charge (one of which Committee is the owner of this estate), to commemorate the first discovery and settlement of America by the Norsemen about the year A.D. 1000.

It is possible that the design of this Norwegian sculptor or that of some other, may be erected in some form on camp John Adams, in the spring of 1878 or before.

It is now well established that the Norsemen visited our American Continent long before the time of Columbus; coasting down from Greenland, passing along Cape Cod, through Vineyard Sound, to Narragansett Bay, in our Commonwealth of Massachusetts.

Leif Ericson, son of Eric the Red, discovered, named and landed at Vineland (now Martha's .Vineyard) in the year A.D. 1000. It was so named from the profusion of grape-vines there found. He built houses, and wintered at Leifsbooths.

He returned to Greenland in 1001; and Thorwald borrowed his brother Leif's ship and landed at Leifsbooths, and passed the winter of 1002–3.*

Thorstein, Eric's third son, fitted out the same ship to bring back the body of his brother. His wife Goodrida went with him; a storm drove them to Greenland, where he died, and his wife returned to Ericsford. She married Thorfinn, a wealthy man of illustrious lineage, and persuaded him to undertake a voyage, and establish a colony in Vineland. He arrived with 160 colonists at Leifsbooths-Hòp (now Mt. Hope Bay, Massachusetts), in 1007. In 1008 Goodrida gave birth to a son, who received the name of Snorre.

Bishop Thorlak, who was the son of the daughter of this Snorre, was born A.D. 1085, and died A.D. 1133. He is reported as the probable author of the Icelandic Sagas, which give an account of these discoveries, which were written *and on record* in the twelfth century (more than three hundred years previous to the landing of Columbus.

---

* Thorwald was killed by an arrow at Kialarnes (Keel Cape, or Cape Cod) in the summer of 1004, in a fight with the Esquimau Indians who then roamed in these regions. He was buried at a place called, at his dying request, *Crossness*.

There was found in Fall River, about the beginning of the present century, a human skeleton, encased in armor, supposed by many to be that of Thorwald. Longfellow has immortalized this by his poem " The Skeleton in Armor."

The minute exactness of the record, giving the time of the rising and setting of the sun, variations of high and low water, the rapidity of the currents, the outlines of the coast, the naming of many places by the Norwegian word Holl (hill), which has been corrupted to Hole — as Woods' Hole — the number of days' sail from Greenland, and other conclusive evidences, have proved to the satisfaction of all historians that the hardy and roving Norwegians first settled North America, and that our good *old* Commonwealth of Massachusetts has the honor of having received the first imprints of European civilization. It is therefore OUR DUTY, and we of Massachusetts should take the initiatory step towards the erection of a Memorial Monument to these hardy *voyageurs.*

The inscriptions cut on the famous Dighton Rock, which is submerged at high tide in the Taunton River, have been by some historians regarded as Runic characters; among them Prof. Rafn, of Copenhagen, the distinguished Runic scholar, who translated a part of them to read " Thorfinn with 151 men took possession of this country." The Icelandic Sagas record that 9 of the 160 colonists separated from the company. But far the larger number of those whose researches are worthy of credence, hold to the opinion that these hieroglyphics are of Indian origin, many similar to them having been found in the Middle and

Western States. Drawings of these inscriptions are found in the "*Antiquitates Americanæ.*"

The first known copy of this inscription was made by Dr. Danforth in 1680, followed by Cotton Mather's in 1712; Dr. Greenwood's in 1730, and by numerous others in the 18th and the present centuries.

Whatever the origin of this Dighton Rock, it is one of the oldest archæological relics of our country, and as such should be preserved from the abrasion of the tides and from vandalism.

The Dighton Rock, and the land about it, was purchased by Neils Arnzen, a Norwegian residing in Fall River, at the request of Ole Bull, and deeded to the Royal Society of Antiquarians of Copenhagen, of which the King of Denmark is the active president, who had expressed a decided interest in its preservation.

This Society has recently signified its willingness to assign all its rights to a Committee of Bostonians consisting of Thomas G. Appleton, Rev. E. E. Hale, Prof. E. N. Horsford, Curtis Guild, Percival L. Everett and Wm. E. Baker, who solicit funds from those interested —

First, for the erection in Boston of a Memorial Monument to the Norsemen;

Secondly, for the preservation of the Dighton Rock as a valuable archæological relic, be it Indian or Runic.

In this Union Monument will be found (and, until
it is finished, in the boat-house) a large oil-painting of
" The Ambuscade of the Racketers by the Pillow Brigade."
This scene represents a night ever memorable to those in
camp John Adams at the time of the Fraternal Welcome
Fête. One portion of the camp formed a Racket Club,
whose duties were to assemble at midnight and keep the
rest of the camp from sleep the remainder of the night;
and they succeeded admirably until, on the night of Monday, July 10, the Club, armed with two hundred wood rat-
tles, sixty large brass bells and numerous tin horns, were
returning, about midnight, from giving a serenade to the
South Carolina ladies in the " Singed-Cat Cottage," when
they were surprised by all the rest of the camp, under
the command of Major W. T. Geary and Judge H. D. D.
Twiggs, of Augusta, Ga. ; D. P. Robertson, of Charleston,
S. C., commanding the centre; and the right wing under
that of George B. Edwards, of Charleston, and of "Chap-
lain" Hall, better known as " the gentleman from North
Carolina."

This ambuscade force had armed themselves with their
bed-pillows, and hid behind the walls by the roadside.
The surprise was complete. The thuds of the pillows
descending upon the heads of the Racketers, was the first
notice of the attack, and the Racketers soon measured their

length and left their impressions in the mud on the road. Recovering somewhat, they however rose to the emergency and captured many pillows; but in the dark, having no distinguishing badge, all those having pillows were regarded as opponents, and thus many Racketers were fiercely contending with their own party. The contest raged fiercely for twenty minutes. The prostrate Racketers rolled the mud hard and dry. The ground was strewn with rackets, bells and tin horns. The Pillow Brigade finally conquered — but only for that night.

The host finally converted the Racketers into A-Rousing Band, to give early matinée concerts, and arouse the camp for breakfast.

Their work on the morning of the Floral and other days of that fête, will be recorded in the "Fétes at Ridge Hill Farms."

In the basement of this UNION MONUMENT HEADQUARTERS (which measures 25 x 60 feet), are two targets, one of an Indian, life size, who, upon being shot in the heart, raises his tomahawk, and the other of a female who beats a tattoo on a large drum.

Here also are to be set thirty-six of Busch's improved magnifying stereoscopes, the invention of Frederic Busch, a native of Prussia, but adopting Boston as his home, who, without professing any knowledge of optics, has dis-

covered and proved the fallacy of many theories hitherto
unquestioned. The valuable collections of objects, num-
bering nearly two thousand selections, in natural history,
&c., have also been secured, but these latter for the
School of Microscopy to be established in November next
at the Boston Aquarium, 13 West Street.

In this monument will be seen a large painting, measuring 7 x 13 feet, portraying in front of the State House,
Boston, a black sow — symbol of that one found astray in
the streets of Boston in 1636 — the litigation concerning
which was the direct cause of the organization of the higher
branch of the Legislature, known as the Senate of Massachusetts, which was the first Senate organized in the
United States. Gathered around the pig are seen many of
the prominent makers of history in the times of the old
Massachusetts Bay Colony in the 17th and 18th centuries.
Those in the foreground include the following : —

GOVERNORS OF MASSACHUSETTS.

John Winthrop, who held office 1630-1633; 1637-1639;
1642-1643; 1646-1648.

Henry Vane, 1636.

John Endicott, 1644, 1649; 1655-1664.

John Leverett, 1673-1678.

Simon Bradstreet, 1676-1686.

Joseph Dudley, 1702, 1714.

William Burnett, 1728.

John Hancock, 1780–1785; 1787–1793.

Samuel Adams, 1794–1797.

AND

Edward Winslow,	born 1594, died 1655.	
John Davenport,	1597,	1669.
Thomas Prince,	1600.	1673.
John F. Winthrop, F.R.S.,	1638,	1707.
John Cotton, LL.D.,	1638,	1699.
Increase Mather, D.D.,	1639,	1723.
Cotton Mather, D.D., F.R.S.,	1663,	1728.
Benj. Coleman,	1673,	1747.
William Coleman,	1688,	1729,
James Otis,	1725,	1783.*
Gen. Benj. Lincoln,	1733,	1810.
Charles Chauncey, LL.D.,	1747,	1822.

Here will also be found, when finished by the artist sculptor, Herbert Gleason, of Boston, a group representing " *Our Old Mother Eve* " as *Pomona*, presenting a crown-wreath of laurel, and an apple of gold on a salver — emblem of the knowledge of Good and Evil — to one of Massachusetts' most genial and distinguished citizens,

---

* James Otis was born in Boston, in the year A.D. 1725. As an orator he had to a remarkable extent that animal magnetism which electrified citizens of his time to valient acts. He was killed by lightning, in A.D. 1783, while standing in the doorway of his home.

who for many, many years has been endorsed all over the
country by his continued re-election as the President of
the American Pomological Society.

When the world shall have ceased to relish the apple,
queen of fruits, then only shall the world cease to vener-
ate Marshall P. Wilder, founder of the American Pomological Society, for many years President of the Massachusetts Horticultural Society and of the Historic-Gene-
alogical Society; a stiring, effective and reliable man in aid-
ing with his magnetic powers all that pertains to history,
science, or the fruits of life. Brillart Saverin, writes
that he who discovers a new dish is greater than he who
discovers a new planet. Marshall P. Wilder's aim in life
has been nobly accomplished. No man more than he has
trained and improved the fruits of our land, and has made
them luscious, beautiful and invigorating. Commendation is ever in place for those whose life is so monumen-
talized as no marble can make it, by the acts of these
apostles to the doctrine, " By faith and works shall they
know us."

Reader, what are *you* good for? What have *you* done?
What will *you* do to prove that you are of any worth in
this world of ours? Are you contented to prove yourself
as only of the fungus order, rising one day and rotting
the next? *Nous verrons.*

Here also are found several games, including skittles, toss-ball, &c., which, whenever the convenience of the owner will allow, can, upon application at the Registry Office, be used, the fees for their use to be applied to the within-specified charity; but the use of the table games in the Tivoli Hall or of the Bowling Alley are exclusively for the guests of the proprietor. and all *considerate* visitors will please DISCIPLINE all such as disregard this restriction and meddle with them.

On the right of Sunset Slope is the Chilian Pavilion, from the Philadelphia Centennial; its sixteen arches representing the sixteen departments in Chili.

On or about this site in 1872 were four large barns and other farm accessories. These were moved away, herd-yards filled, slopes graded. and the five grass-sod Terraces, four hundred feet in length. formed. On reaching the Octagon Bear-Pit turn to the left — south — down to Terrace Avenue. Turn to the right on Terrace Avenue to the *Gnome Drinking Fountain* at the base of the Bear Pit.*

Looking west toward the water of Sabrina Lake you see Swan Island, one half acre, and on it the little church marked, on its roof, " The Church for good little ducks."

---

* Gentlemen's Walk at the junction of Sunset Slope and Terrace Avenues.

Ladies' Cottage — Terrace Avenue near Octagon Bear-Pit.

Turn into the footpath by the ARBORETUM KNOLL to
the *Arboretum Basin*, which is built of red brick, sixty
feet in diameter; it is encircled with a three-inch copper
tube, so pierced that eight hundred fine jets of water can
be ejected, curving upward and inwardly towards the
Spray Fountain; which fountain, when in play, throws
five hundred jets curving outwardly.   These thirteen hundred jets form one combined mass of water, spray and
mist, sixty feet in diameter and forty feet in height, which
in the sunlight shows the colors of the rainbow.   The
fountain is fifteen feet in height, with four basins, one
above the other; between the first and second basins are
grouped four statues, as follows : Powers' *Greek Slave*,
Thorwaldsen's *Venus*, Pradier's *Venus*, and *Urania*.

Between the second and third basins there are three metal
Amphytrions from the balcony of the Boston Theatre;
above the third basin is a group with Hebe pitchers.

Pass this Spray Fountain, and follow the footpath by
the side of the ARBORETUM KNOLL to the Arboretum
Lodge, constructed of many thousands of small rounds
of cedar (stop and count them).   Descend the steps of the
Arboretum Lodge to the edge of the lake, and, looking
back to the west side of Arboretum Knoll, there can be
seen, placed upon two dead limbs of a tree, three
small Churches for swallows and other birds, which

are marked, according to their respective elevation, "*High Church*," "*Middle Church*," "*Low Church*," — "*all on the same root.*" Crossing Arboretum Lodge bridge, the visitor reaches *Tri-Pont* (three bridge) Island, two acres in area; its second being the RUSTIC BRIDGE at the north end, and its third, the COLISEUM BRIDGE, one hundred and sixty feet long, at the west side. This latter bridge is so named because the heavy timber composing it was first used by the city of Boston in constructing the temporary bridges over the Providence Railroad connecting Dartmouth and Berwick Park Streets with the Peace Jubilee Coliseum of 1872.

In the Medallions on the south side of this Coliseum Bridge are the heads of *Apollo* and *Diana*, and on the north side those of Ariadne and Silenus.*

The granite curbing of the basin for the Frog Fountain

---

* The latter a semi-god, the nurse, the preceptor and the attendant of Bacchus, who was very fond of him. Midas, King of Thracia, captured him once and put various questions to him, among others, "What is best for men?" After a long silence he received for answer, "Life is most free from pain when one is ignorant of future evils. It is best of all for man not to be born; the second is for those who are born to die as soon as possible."

For releasing him Bacchus promised Midas to grant any request which he chose to ask. Midas craved that all he touched might turn to gold; but was glad to have that power revoked when he found himself on the point of starving.

on this Tri-Pont Island originally formed three enclosures in front of the Masonic Temple, Boston, corner of Tremont and Boylston Streets.

The BOAT-HOUSE, 20x30 feet, on Tri-Pont Island is made from the ornamental Gothic shelving ordered for the St. George Café, Masonic Temple, Boston. The architect who originated the design did not recognize his own work in its adaptation by the removal of the shelving and using the Gothic frame as the side-walls of the Boat-house.

This Boat-house has two niches on each of three sides, for which statues of appropriate size not being readily attainable, the owner solved the difficulty by selecting subjects from an Art book, and had his artist sketch and his carpenter cut the outline from boards. These were painted and shaded in relief so that this board statuary is quite deceptive.

On the east or water-end of the Boat-house there are three doors for the exit and admission of the boats; two niches with fret-saw statuary, Italianized, of PSYCHE Meditive, and CLIO; and seven oil-paintings, representing —

The Frog Concert on an English Steamship.

Moonlight Courtship in the Gondola. The Hog dressed as the Doge of Venice, accompanied by his Pig page descending the palace steps to his gondola.

Penelope, Cinderella, Sappho and *Silenus.*

On the south side in the two niches, *Melpomene* and the Lute-player.

On the six panels: — Bears as Italian *pifferari*, the female bear dressed in Albanian costume, dancing the tarantella.

Thomas Cat inviting Mrs. Pussy to a boat-ride on Sabrina Lake.

Descent from Olympus, Desolation, Fortuna, and Venus rising from the Sea.

On the west end or land entrance are two panel paintings; one showing the HYDROPATHIC TREATMENT, by an upset on Sabrina Lake, and the other " *The taking of the Sun (observations) on an English Ocean Steamship.* "

On the north side, in the two niches, Bayadere and Ganymede; and on the seven panels, *Nereide riding on a Ram of the Golden Fleece*, Twilight, Dawn of Morning, Cupid drawn by two Deer, *Meum et Tuum*, or the bather who saved his shirt and is anxious to give the monkeys *fits* who borrowed his boat and clothing.

Bruin's Separation from his Bear-wife when going to Sea with his Green Umbrella. The Arrival of the Irishman, Scotchman, Englishman and Yankee.

The Yankee, of course, is the *first ashore*, and tb't before the hawsers of the steamship are made fast. He takes a bold step, as if he *knew* just where he was going.

The Scotchman strokes his beard, and methodically plans his departure, from which an earthquake or a volcanic eruption can divert him only long enough to *calculate* the loss by the desolation, and how much he can get by a sale of the *débris*.

The Irishman waits to find where the others go, and then he means to follow, hunt up a drap of "mountain dew," help build a church, and remit funds to bring over the "rist of the family."

The Englishman is in no hurry to move. He contemplates the fact that he *has* arrived, and wonders where the best chop-house is to be found. He is aware that the Yankees are a wonderfully ingenious and driving people, but thinks they don't always know " how best to do it." He wants to start a general-improvement stock company to utilize the sewerage of Boston for the production of choice grapes and strawberries-and-cream, rather than throw it away where the incoming tide will wash more or less of it in lodgments on South Boston Flats, and give the deadhead co-associate contemplaters on Noddle's Island and in the City Government (for 1877 only) another chance to deadhead citizens, this time in new hospitals and lovely cemeteries.

On the roof of the Boat-house are two Lions, ornated with gold-leaf: these were once the property of Francis L. Peabody, of Salem.

The inside of the Boat-house is temporarily floored over, and on the side-walls are various comical engravings, portraying fishes, fishermen and boatmen.

But of all the numerous improvements accomplished at Ridge Hill Farms, that of the greatest magnitude is the making of the artificial Lake Sabrina.

Finding, in 1871, a spring near the site of the Boat-house, the owner excavated and formed a small pond 200 feet in diameter. He extended this, in 1873, to the large weeping elm tree, and built the stone lock with two gates, now covered by the *Rustic Bridge*, intending to form another pond on the north side. The springs here were found more powerful, and as the water-sheds from the high lands naturally incited the task, the work was extended, and in 1874, 1875 and 1876 the northern, western and southern dykes were completed and stone-banked and the artificial lake finished, which is nearly one and one half miles in circuit, and varies from four to twenty-two feet in depth. Sabrina Lake is thirty-five feet above the level of Charles River. It is fed by springs, water-sheds, a six-inch pipe, over one mile in length, to other springs, and by the overflow from the high-service Water Tower.

It was stocked with black bass in 1874, which fish and horn-pout have rapidly multiplied.

It has three islands, of which Tri-pont is the largest, two acres, Oak Island at the north end, about one acre, the second, and Swan Island, one-half acre, west of Arboretum Knoll. On this Lake are Muscovy and Aylesbury ducks, black and white swans, thirteen row-boats, a fleet of toy ships, and a small steamboat, six feet in length, complete in all its appointments, built by a deaf mute in Boston, who spent twelve months in its construction. The works are of brass and copper, and have the capacity to run thirty minutes with one firing.

Leave TRI-PONT ISLAND by the covered RUSTIC BRIDGE, and pass to the base of the CIRCULAR BEAR-PIT, built of red brick in 1875, thirty-two feet in diameter; thence return to the Rocky Avenue and the Steamboat Pier. "THE LADY OF THE LAKE," here found, is fifty feet in length, and will carry forty passengers. It was built on the place, and is propelled in the water by floats attached to endless chains, in place of the usual side-wheels. By running the steamboat on to a truck-frame with wheels submerged in the water, then disconnecting the motor from the endless chain floats and connecting to the driving wheels of the truck, it can be propelled on a tramway. The increased size of Sabrina Lake, however, avoids the necessity of connecting it by tramways to Charles River, as was at first projected. This amphibious steamboat was launched on Charity Day, July 14, 1876, of the Fraternal Welcome Fête.

From the Steamboat Pier continue north up Rocky Avenue to the *Peacock House*, which will be found at the junction of Krino Avenue. Looking south on Krino Avenue you see THE BOSTON FIRE MONUMENT, composed of the only four granite columns of the new Boston post-office injured by the great fire of November 10, 1872. The arched iron girders tying these columns are surmounted at the apex by a revolving statue of *Mercury*.

All the Elm and Pine trees found near this Fire Monument and the Peacock House have been moved about one mile and here replanted since September, 1875. They vary in height from thirty to seventy feet. The total number of trees, small and large, planted or transplanted on the estate, since September, 1875, will aggregate over three thousand.

Near the Peacock House will be found the *Deer Park*. In this enclosure will be found two elks from Nebraska, named *Stag-horn Elkie* and *Nebraska Fanny;* three deer, one a fallow or spotted deer from England, named *Cousin Fanny*, another from the State of Maine, called *Maine-nie-Deer*, and *Deer-rie Orleans*, who ran into New Orleans as her city of refuge at the time of the last flood — not that of Noah's time, but that of the Brashear crevasse.

The brown and white antelope from Colorado is called *Nebraska Dickey*, and his goat lady-love, *Nancy White*.

The male bison is from Colorado, and is called *Buffalo Bob Haycock*, in honor of Buffalo Bill (Haycock), the famous trapper — not he that is playing at the theatres — who first lassoed him.

The female bison (by many called buffalo, though incorrectly unless preceded by the word American) was captured in Kansas, and was by the trappers named *Julia*, to which the present owner added the name of *Sweeny*, in honor of Mr. John Sweeny, of Sandusky, Ohio, who organized the expedition of eleven trappers which caught *Bob Haycock*, and, after a three days' chase, *Pompey Haycock*, the largest buffalo and evidently the king of the herd, who died this early spring by striking his head against the log corrall of his winter-quarters when the attendants were attempting to ring his nose.

Pass northerly on the Krino Avenue to the Archway marked KRINO VALLEY *of Fancies, Follies and Frivolities.**

**Krino* (Greek), to order, inquire and search into; investigate; to distinguish between good and bad; *i.e.*, criticising judgment.

The numerous comical peculiarities of this place are sufficiently explicit, and do not require any description in this guide. They should be *seen* to be fully appreciated. A printed description first read of many of them would be tame, and destroy half the surprise controlling the visitor to the quaint *make-ups* here gathered.

Attention. however, may here be called to the Tarpeian Rock. just at the entrance arch, the Race Horses, the Bottle Monument to "The Departed Spirits," *John Soulier's* Epitaph, which reads as follows : " To the memory of John Soulier, boot-maker. He was a man of great under-standing, and knew best how to treat corned feet. Not-a bene : the best way to stretch boots is to fill them with beans, then water and let 'em swell. His widow, a blonde, aged 27, continues at the old stand, and makes a specialty of giving fits to children and widowers." Also The Darwinian Theory, the Little Fawns from Boston Common. who died while fawning around city officials, Billy Bruin's Chaplet, containing the great Black Bear. taxidermisted, which escaped from Ridge Hill Farms in July, 1874. just as he had arrived there, and who roamed about for ten days. to the dismay of residents within a circuit of fifty miles, by his scratchin g at their doors at midnight hours, seeking table dainties, upon which this tame Bear had been fed. The daily reports in the Bos-

ton newspapers, of Billy Bruin's visits to houses at
night, and churches on Sundays, &c., to avoid his
pursuers, of his maiming human species, swallowing
babies, &c., &c., caused great fear among the credu-
lous and timid believers, until he was reported as
wounded at North Weymouth, and the next morning his
body found floating near the beach at Hull. Numerous
readers of the Boston newspapers will recall the funeral
obsequies of Billy Bruin at Ridge Hill Farms on July 8,
and that of the Swan Leander on July 19, 1874, killed by
the alligator.

Many of the one thousand invited guests present sent
laments in prose or rhyme pertaining to Bears or Swans.
One from Dr. Oliver Wendell Holmes reads as follows : —

"296 BEACON SREET, Aug. 1, 1874.

"Dear Sir, — Many thanks for your polite invitation to
attend the obsequies of the lamented plantigrade. I am
sorry that it will not be in my power to be present upon the
melancholy occasion. I have a great respect for bears
since those two female ones taught the little children of
Bethel and of Belial that they must not be rude to elderly
persons. I think a loose bear or two might be of service
in our community, and I regret much the loss of an ani-

mal who might have done so much as a moral teacher for the young of this city and its suburbs.

> "I am, dear sir, yours very truly,
>
> "O. W. HOLMES."

The small (?) Farmer's Boy on the hill has a pretty smile. "*The representative of the 'Hub' or modern Athens*" has a wise look, derived, probably, from his ancestors, the "Greek Roots," or *Grecian Benders*, so curiously humanized on Oak Island.

"One of the Kentucky Bourbons" looks tipsy, and has a *rye* face. The negro has lost part of his pipe of peace, and found a piece of pipe. The interior of the "Diggers' Retreat," shingled with old picks, spades and shovels. used up in making Lake Sabrina, causes all to smile "out loud." This part is thus explained: —

> "SACRED 2 THE MEMORY
>
> Of those who for 3 years have been digging! — *digging!!* — DIGGING!!! — these Canals, Ponds and Lakes; who, standing in the water, got very wet, and yet frequently *persisted* that they were very *dry!*
>
> "If you use a little blarney, and give them plenty of
> rations,
> These lovers of the Green(s), they can just bate all nations
> In the use of the pick and the shovel.

"On pipes the Dutch may possibly bate the Irish a wee bit,
But they never can smoke out of them — a bit of their wit.
"No! no! ould Ireland's always ready for a lark,
As in classics it is certainly quite up to the mark;
For you may 'get the best' dictionary and sarch it clane
      through,
You may torture your brain until all is sky blue,
But surely, 'when Greek meets Greek,' must mane
That the Emerald *I'le* is just like *warm* Greece — that's
      plane."

The large Hog, standing upright on his hind feet under
the ornamental wood frame, was erected on June 19, 1875,
at the fête frolic given to Southern guests at the time of
their visiting Boston to participate in the Bunker Hill
Centennial; it is marked, on one side, "*Massachusetts
Senate*, 1636, *Sow*." On the other side, "*Japhet in search
of his* —— *Alma Mater*."

This Monument is to commemorate the circumstances
which led to the organization of the higher branch of the
Legislature or Senate of Massachusetts, the history of
which, by Winthrop, Palfrey, and others, is thus recorded:

There was a stray sow found in the streets of Boston
in the year A.D. 1636. It was brought to Captain Keayne,
a man of property and consequence (he was one of the

founders of the Ancient and Honorable Artillery Company, in 1638), but he was unpopular for alleged hardness in dealings. He gave public notice about finding the sow, by the town crier and otherwise, but no claimant appeared for nearly a year, until after he had killed a pig of his own which had been kept along with the stray sow; then the Widow Sherman came to see it, and not being able to identify it with the one which she had lost, alleged that the slaughtered pig was hers. The Elders of the Church of Boston, after hearing the parties, exonerated Captain Keayne. The Widow Sherman was dissatisfied, and brought her case to trial before a jury, who decided for the defendant. Then Keayne sued the Widow for defamation in charging him with theft, and recovered forty pounds damages. Mrs. Sherman was not satisfied yet, and appealed to the General Court or Legislature in 1642. This body was composed of magistrates and deputies, who sat and voted in the same chamber. The wrangling over the rehearing of the case occupied seven days. Then two magistrates and fifteen deputies voted for a reversal of the previous decision, and seven magistrates and eight deputies voted in approval of it; the other seven deputies stood doubtful.

Thus a large majority of the superior officers was for one party, while on a joint vote the majority of the court

would be for the other. Therefore the case was not deter-
mined, and there also arose the very important question
of the relation of the magistrates appointed by the Charter
Company, who were more or less subject to the crown in-
fluence, and that of the deputies elected by the popular
vote. After long contention, the publication of a *brochure*
concerning the hog dispute, and a special proclamation by
the Governor, John Winthrop, the negative voice of the
magistrates was overruled, and as a sequence came the
organization of the higher branch, elected by the popular
vote, henceforth known as the Senate.

The dedicatory speech at the time of the erection of this
Senate Monument, was made by J. F. C. Hyde, Esq.,
who was President of the Senate in 1869-70.

The 1812 War Hog Monument was dedicated June 19,
1875, with a speech by Governor Howard, of Rhode Isl-
and. Tradition thus tells us that which has its earnest
and decided believers and unbelievers :

By the carelessness of a boy in 1811, a garden gate was
left open; two pigs entered and rooted up a few plants.
The owner of the garden, when attempting to drive them
out, had to contend against the well-known obstinacy of that
animal to be *driven* anywhere. They would *not* go out at
the open gate, and finally fell dead exhausted in their race
to keep away from their fierce pursuant. The owner of

the hogs sued the owner of the garden for extreme violence when ejecting them. This engendered a hard feeling, which led the owner of the garden to vote, at the next
election, for the candidate to the United States Senate from
the opposing party for which he had previously voted. This
opposition candidate, Howell, was elected United States
Senator by *one* majority; and the question was put in the
Senate, " Shall the question of war with England be post-
poned to the next session?" This Howell voted No; and
this vote also was decided by (his) one majority. He also
voted *no* on the next question, namely, " Shall war with
England now be declared?" which was carried in the
affirmative: yet his two previous negative votes nullified
his last vote, and caused the war of 1812. Thus the two
hogs who stole into the garden to *search for roots*, by
their resisting expulsion unto their death, caused the
election of Howell, whose negative vote caused war with
England, in 1812, and settled forever the *right of search*
claimed by the English Naval Service over American
ships. This alleged historical fact or tradition has
its believers and its non-believers; but ex-Governor
Howard, and the then Lieut.-Governor (but now Governor) Van Zandt, assert that this hog tradition reads so
prettily that no true son of Little Rhody should be vandal

enough to hunt up evidence to undermine the honors got
by this big result for the little State of Rhode Island.

Returning in the Krino Valley by the same path, the
visitor's attention will be arrested on the lake-side by
numerous ducks, heron, and other feathered species; an
alligator, otter, beaver, &c., so well stuffed that they refuse every dainty offered them. A small sign on one of a
cluster of white-birch trees is marked, " Good for our
boys." " As the twig is bent, the boy's inclined."

Leave Krino Valley by the *Lakeside Path*, which is
just inside of the archway by which you entered; pass the
Rustic Seat Umbrella, south, to the *Gothic Arch*, which
formed the main entrance to the Presbyterian Church,
corner of Beach Street and Harrison Avenue, that was
partially destroyed by the Globe Theatre district fire on
May 29, 1873, and afterwards taken down by the city of
Boston in order to widen the street. Through this *Arch*
we reach the *Smugglers' Cove*, the waters of *Lake Sabrina* on one side, and on the other, boulders of rock, piled
high, at much labor and expense, these rocks having
formed division walls of the lowlands and fields now covered by the waters of *Lake Sabrina*. On the right of the
Tunnel entrance is seen the grim form and visage of the
Smuggler Chief, and on the left the *Red-man*, with war
paint and tomahawk. Passing through the rocky subter-

ranean tunnel we reach the *Round Tower*, thirty-five feet in height, its stone walls scintillating with crystals. This Tower was finished about the time of the *Crystal Wedding Fête*, September 20, 1875. After going through the second subterranean passage we reach the SMUGGLERS' CAVE, with high vaulted roof, and huge rocks composing its sides, cut with grotesque and sphinx-like faces; here also are found numerous of the smugglers' captives, among whom are Mrs. Cardiff, Boss Tweed, Punch, four of the Forty Thieves, peeping from Barbara's oil-jars, and the Girl of the Period, with *Ezra Winslow*, the latter of which is placarded as follows: "English officials arrested me, the British Ministry requested my detention. But the Act of Parliament of 1870 released me, thus declaring that I was *wrongfully* arrested and wrongfully detained; *ergo* I have a claim against the British Government of £100,000, which I assign to the Boston Banks, as some satisfaction for not getting my body extradited." In this cave, here and there, from the crevices in the rocks are seen huge hands protruding, apparently to greet you, but showing also their cloven feet. To add to the weird and subterranean influences, the visitors can see, at the furthest southern extremity of this cave, the Black Bears, in the Circular Bear Pit before mentioned, ready to hug them through the iron bars which shut them from the cave.

After viewing the " Rock — a-boy-baby," on the right, about one hundred feet from the southern extremity of the cave, ascend the steps and pass through the long dark *Flirtation Tunnel.* Here every gentleman offers his hand to some lady — to guide her underground. This hand-in-hand walk of faith below, makes light of the darkness, and leaves pleasant impressions for long after, the world above is reached.

The timid may rest assured that there is nothing to cause alarm anywhere in these caverns or subterranean tunnels. It may be noticed that in arranging his grounds, the proprietor locates everything pertaining to the same class or special kind of attraction or amusement, by itself, in one section; and does not, unless some peculiarity of nature specially tempts him, scatter in different parts of the estate his mushroom growth of varied surprises.

Thus the timid visitor need not fear to pass all alone through the Flirtation Tunnel. The surprise experienced on reaching the STALACTITE GROTTO will amply compensate for and brighten the imagination of any clouded by the darkness in the Tunnel. The rays of the sun when not too low in the horizon, entering through the colored glasses in the roof of the Grotto, which is just above the surface of the ground, reflect all the hues of the rainbow upon the stalactites pendent from the roof.

The serpentine paths of this grotto are covered with white marble dust; it has eight miniature lakes stocked with gold and silver fish. The *Amethyst Lake* is so named from the water spraying into the basin having the appearance of that jewel when the sun is high enough to reflect its rays through the roof opening. The water passes from *Amethyst Lake* into *Lake Crystal,* thence into two huge shells from Calcutta, overflowing from the flutes into the *Fluted Shell Lake.*

The water from *Diana's Pool,* at the south end of the Grotto, rushes in small streams through crevices and over the rocks, and in grooves in the stone, dashing against shells and other obstructions, falling clear and sparkling into the Devil's Basin, where the thirsty are tempted to stop and drink.

The roof of this Grotto is supported by seven stone columns which were once the pinnacles of the same church as the *Gothic Arch.*

The crystalline and conch-shell arches, the rose-colored shells, the prismatic hues upon the cubes and flakes of glass clustered around the lake borders, with the entwining and other vines; the fern fronds, the intricate windings, the rugged ascents and descents, and the music of the falling waters, idealize the romance of fiction.

These subterranean chambers are inaccessible to frost,

and thus the work of construction has been continued all the winter months.

The vandalism of many visitors, in breaking off and carrying away shells and crystals, are sore trials of patience to the owner and his superintendent, who have passed many midnight hours planning and arranging them.

The apparently uncontrollable propensity of visitors to carry away souvenirs is very costly and annoying. Quoting from the daily reports for the past month of July, one of the inspectors, while secreted in the Grotto for one half-hour, observed twenty persons, of the one hundred who passed through, possess themselves of shells, crystals, &c. Should one fifth of the visitors to this estate prove thus inconsiderate, the work of restoration must necessarily be constant and costly.

As the visitor leaves the Grotto by the Exit Turnstile, and passes into the outer air, he will note the difference, and appreciate the cooler temperature of his quarter-mile walk under ground.

Follow the Exit path, and down the grassy slope to the **side** of the goat-riders to the Krino Avenue. Thence turn to the left, and pass between the Boston Fire Monument and Circular Bear-Pit, to the CAMERA OBSCURA, on the terrace near Hillside Avenue. The six pillars supporting the roof of this building are from that part of the Old State House removed by the city of Boston in 1876 in order to straighten Devonshire Street.

Upon entering this Dark Chamber, the surrounding landscape will be portrayed upon the round table, perfect in outline, color and movement, by the aid of lenses revolving at the apex of the roof.

Leaving the Camera Obscura, the visitor will pass to the *Photograph Studio*, which is near the Registry Office.

Those who desire to purchase photographic views of the place will ask for a printed slip, and indicate by writing the *number* of each view wanted. This method will save the time and words both of visitors and of attendants.

REMARKS.

It is impossible for any one to visit Ridge Hill Farms, no matter what his tastes, without having the mind directed into new channels, and controlled to think for himself, on returning to his home, of some new departure from the conventionalities and ruts of routine life. If the owner has adopted any rule of action in improving his estate, it seems to be more that of *avoiding* the routine style of all others. He believes that his sphere of action in life is to amuse others, and that a little nonsense now and then is more compatible with the summer recreative season or country life, and tends to direct the mind for a brief space from the thorns and trials common to our daily walks.

The financial expenditures, and the constant application, physically and mentally, for the amusement and benefit of others, would be most appreciably returned by courteous acts of consistency.

Therefore will each visitor *act* as a monitor and disciplinarian toward all who may be seen *trespassing* by

Walking on the grass or flower plots;

Annoying the pet animals with sticks or stones, or by giving them tobacco;

Strewing the ground with refuse paper or garbage from the luncheon basket;

Handling when they should not touch; stealing ornaments from the buildings, or plants, fruits or flowers from the gardens or hot-houses;

Breaking twigs from valuable trees, destroying fern fronds, and that which requires months or years to restore;

Crowding the veranda of the proprietor's residence, and peeping in at the doors or windows;

Or wasting by *talk* the paid hours of the laborers; which, if it does not cease, must result in the employment of such as cannot speak English, that are deaf and dumb or wear anti-hearing ear-pads.

The Registry Office is specially established to respond to all the enquiries concerning the Heavens above, the Earth beneath, and the Waters round about, which many *peculiar* people have been asking at the door of the proprietor's residence, — such as for the loan of tumblers, pitchers of ice-water, parasols, umbrellas, waterproofs, perambulators, tea-spoons, money on chattel mortgages, and for all the charities in the known and unknown regions; restoratives for the faint, halters for horses, and milk for the babies.

Strangers will confer a favor by permitting the proprietor to reserve, EXCLUSIVELY *for his family and guests, the inside of his residence, the veranda, round about, and the driveway on the north side of it.*

Although the proprietor has, upon request, consented to hold SOME horses, his duties are such that he cannot be relied upon to be always on hand for this service.

NOTICE.

In order to save retracing steps, visitors should follow the track as herein consecutively described. It may, however, be stated that that which is on this 1st day of September, may be materially innovated before November, by the restless activity which here prevails and has given use to the *sobriquet* of the " human earthquake."

That which is herein alluded to as projected, may now never be done, inasmuch as the projector has such an aversion to any prior notice of the intention *to do.*

The owner of this estate repudiates all titles, and particularly desires it known that he is not *entitled* to the prefix of *Colonel,* by which many have addressed him since the presentation, by the Fifth Maryland National Guards, of a broken sword with three ribbons attached, which, according to some military regulations, made him *Colonel* by *brevet* of that Regiment. He requires all so calling him to spell it *Kernel.* He believes that only such as *earn* titles are entitled to have them, and therefore he abominates that relic of the country village, the word "Esquire," now so commonly used as the caudal appendage to the name of every man.

Trusting that as you go to your homes, *wherever* they may be, you will be mindful that as you are blessed or are entertained by others, so you should extend to others such comforts and pleasing diversities from mental cares as may be within your province, and hopeful that you will evidence your sympathy in the charities projected in the *addenda* hereinafter, — A Dieu.

Toi-soinez,

PORCUPINE QUILL.

CATALOGUE

OF

Statues, Busts, Vases, Curiosities, &c.

AT THE

RIDGE HILL FARMS.

TRADE MARK

WELLESLEY, MASS.

SEPTEMBER, 1877.

This Swan, in a boat on wheels, drawn by a Turtle, is from the engraving of *The First Hour*, by Raphael. It was adopted as the trademark of Ridge Hill Farms because of the general interpretation that the Turtle is capable of carrying a great weight, and of long-continued work. The Brahmin mythology represented the globe resting on the back of the Turtle — and thus the Turtle, by its accumulated force from a strong will, moved the world, as the mosquito can worry and move the strongest man. So the Turtle, symbolizing what man can do, or should do, toward working out his *aim* in life.

No.

1.   2 Chamois (Wild Goats).   White zinc.   From Berlin.

2. 17 Large Moulded Stone Flower Vases, Roman style.

3. 17 Small　　do.　　do.　　do.

BORDERING CONSERVATORY LAWN.

4. 2 Russian Bloodhounds.　White zinc.　From Berlin.

5. 2 Water Spaniels.　Colored terra-cotta.　From Munich.

6. The Cat Solicitor.　Colored zinc.　From Dresden.

> The legend says: Once upon a time the noble Marquis of Carrabas was convicted of high treason, his estates confiscated and himelf driven into exile. The unhappy man sent letter upon letter, asking pardon, without receiving any answer; the prayers of his oldest and most influential friends were in vain; his two sons whom he sent, one after the other, were not even received by the stern and unrelenting monarch. As a last venture he sent his educated cat, dressed up as an ambassador, with an humble petition praying for grace and mercy. The cat, accompanied by a trustworthy old servant, was received with astonishment at the royal castle, but was allowed free access. The monarch, in a fit of good humor and merriment, was unable to withstand so much perseverance and humility, and granted revocation of the order of condemnation.

7. Statue, Music conquering Force.　Zinc bronze.

8. 10 Green Majolica Flower Urns, with four Handles. From Montpellier, France.

9. Large Greek Vase on Pedestal.　White terra-cotta. From Scotland.

10. Silver Reflecting Globe on Ornamented Iron Stand. From Paris.

11. Diorama.

12. Swings, exclusively for guests of the proprietor. Visitors using them, or any of the games in Tivoli Hall, will display a sorry return for the courtesies extended in permitting them to visit the estate.

13a. Drinking Fountain, " Leaky Boot." Zinc bronze. From Berlin.

> The basin of this fountain is a fine specimen of quartz rock. It was owned and used by Dr. Morton when making his anæs-thetics.

14. Iron Mortar used in the Confederate Service.

15. Cherubs Playing on a Lyre.

16. 12 " Mushroom " Seats. From French Department Centennial Exhibition.

17. Roman Vase. White zinc.

18. Statue on Pedestal, Flora. By Wittig. Black terra-cotta. From Italian Department Centennial Exhibition.

19. Statue on Pedestal, Asia. By Tondeur. White terra-cotta. From Italian Department Centennial Exhibition.

20. Statute on Pedestal, Africa. By Tondeur. Black terra-cotta. From Italian Department Centennial Exhibition.

21. 2 Green Japanese Seats. Porcelain.

22. 1 Mottled   do.   do.

23. 2 Modern Seats, Imitation Wooden Stumps. Porcelain.

24. Minnehaha's Wigwam.

Containing a series of 8 paintings depicting the course of Intemperance. To change the pictures in the stereoscope of Minnehaha, press on the two buttons.

25. Walter's Garden.

26. Statue on Pedestal, Autumn. By Wittig. Red terra-
cotta. From Italian Department Centennial Exhibition.

27. Eddie's and Walter's Play and Ware House.

28. Eddie's Garden.

29. Statue on Pedestal, Evangeline. Red terra-cotta.
From Italian Department Centennial Exhibition.

30. Statue on Pedestal, Europe. By Tondeur. White
terra-cotta. From Italian Department Centennial
Exhibition.

31. Statue on Pedestal, Psyche. By Thorwaldsen.
White terra-cotta. From Italian Department
Centennial Exhibition.

PAVILION AVENUE,
West Side.

32. 9 Rustic Seats, Imitation Stumps of Trees. Colored
terra-cotta.

33. Chinese Joss (Idol). White marble.

34. A Chinese God. Wood, gilded. Said to be *Diabutus*, and to have been idolized for five hundred years.

35. Cats in Council. Black and white zinc. From Vienna.

36. Statue on Pedestal, Gladiator Borghese. Zinc bronze. Original in Rome.

37. 2 Antique Marble Lions, dormant.

38. 1 Silver Reflecting Globe on Ornamented Iron Stand. From Paris.

39. Antelope. Colored zinc.

40. Triple Cushion Seat. Colored terra-cotta. From Florence.

41. Faun, dormant.   do.   do.

42. 2 Japanese Flower Vases on Pedestals. Colored porcelain.

43. 2 Gnomes. Red terra-cotta. From Bonn, Germany.

44. Triple Cushion Seat. Colored terra-cotta. From Florence.

45. Faun, standing.   do.   do.

46. 2 Statues, Atalanta and Meilanion. White zinc.

Atalanta is recorded in Greek mythology as the daughter of Iasos, King of Arcadia, who, having prayed to the gods for a son, was displeased at her birth, and as a mark of his displeasure, exposed her on the Parthenon mount.

Here she was nurtured by a she-bear, and grew up to womanhood, still, however, retaining her virginity, and becoming the most swift-footed of mortals. She vanquished the Centaurs, who sought to capture her, participated in the Calydonian boar-hunt, and engaged in the Pelian games. In course of time, her father was reconciled to her and restored her filial rights to her. But when he urged her to choose a husband, she insisted that every suitor who aspired to win her should first contend with her in running. If he vanquished her, he was to receive her hand as the prize of the victory; and if vanquished, he was to be put to death.

Meilanion overcame her by practising the following artifice: As he ran, he dropped three golden apples, the gift of Venus, one after the other, along the course, which so fascinated Atalanta that she could not refrain from delaying to pick them up; and while she thus delayed, Meilanion gained the race and a wife. And they lived happy ever after, until they were struck by lightning — by Jupiter — for disobeying his commands.

47. Antelope. Stuffed.
48. Elk. do.

FLORAL ART GARDEN,
Balustrade.

49. Blue Majolica Vase with Goat Handles and Oak-leaf Pedestal.
50. 2 Ornamental Japanese Vases. Porcelain.
51. do. Urn Vases, Chinese Decorations. Terre-cuit. From Italian Department, Centennial.
52. Statue, Boy with Squirrel. Zinc. Italian Department, Centennial.
53. Statue, Boy blowing Bubbles. Rogers.

54. Statue, The Dying Indian Warrior. By P. Stephenson. White marble.

55. Flower Vase. Porcelain.

56. Statue, Shepherd-boy Flute Player. Terre-cuit.

57. 2 Large Etruscan Vases. Terre-cuit. Bronzed.

58. Statue, Flora. Zinc bronze. Italian Department, Centennial. ,

59. Statue, Bacchante. Bronze.

60. Ornamental Porcelain Seat. Chinese.

61. Statue, The Fisher Girl. Terra-cotta. Italian Department, Centennial, Philadelphia.

62. Majolica Vases on Majolica Pedestal. Harvest Gleaners. Wheat and Corn Ornaments. English.

63. Roman Fluted Vase. Majolica. English.

64. Statue, Girl caressing Dog. Zinc. Rhine.

65. do. Girl feeding Pet Eagle. Zinc. Rhine.

66. Greek Fluted Vase. White terra-cotta.

67. Statue, Shepherd Boy. Zinc. Berlin.

68. Ornamental Majolica Vase. England.

NICHES IN GARDEN TRELLIS.

69. Japanese Pedestals. Porcelain.

70. Bust, George Washington. Cast, on Pedestal.

71. Statue, Cupid, Silence, Antique. do. do.

72. do. Diana de Gabia. Terra-cotta.

73. Statue, Ceres. Zinc.
74. Bust, Venus de Milo. Cast, on Pedestal.

FLORAL ART GARDEN,

South Division.

75. Greek Vase with Handles. On Pedestal. White terra-cotta.
76. Fluted Roman Vase. White terra-cotta.
77. do. do.
78. Fountain. Boy and Girl Courtship under Umbrella. Red terre-cuit. Italian Department, Centennial.
79. Medallion Vase with Handles. Elaborate. Terra-cotta. Rhine.
80. Etruscan Medallion Urn. Snake and Eagle Head Handles. Rhine.
81. Flower Urn. Medusa Head Handles. On bronze Pedestal. Terra-cotta. Rhine.
82. Flower Vase. Ornamented. Terra-cotta. Rhine.
83. Flower Urn. Dragon Handles. Terra-cotta Pedestal. Rhine.
84. Statue, Jubilating Faun. Black terra-cotta.
85. Fluted Roman Vase. White terra-cotta.
86. Japanese Flower Stands. Colored porcelain.
87. Seat, Griffins. Terra-cotta. From Rhine.

83. Greek Vase, Grapes. White terra-cotta. From
    Rhine.

89. 2 Statues, Bacchante. Black terra-cotta.

90. Japanese Seat. Lattice. Porcelain.

91. 2 Japanese Pedestals. Quaint Tentacular four-toed
    and Scaly Dragons. Highly illuminated.

92. Greek Vase. White terra-cotta.

93. Ornamented Grape Vase. Black bronze, on Pedestal.
    From Rhine.

94. Ornamented Grape Vase.   do.   do.
    From Rhine.

95. Vine and Grape Vase. White terra-cotta, on Fluted
    Pedestal. From Rhine.

96. Statue, Hercules and the Nemean Lion. Terra-
    cotta. Italian Department.

97. Florentine Vase. Terra-cotta, on Granite Pedestal.
    Italian Department.

98. Group. Trions playing with Dolphins. Red terra-
    cotta. Italian Department.

99. Fluted Roman Vase. White terra-cotta. From
    Scotland.

100. Fluted Roman Vase. White terra-cotta, on Pedestal.
     From Scotland.

101. Etruscan Vase. White terra-cotta. From Scotland.

102. 2 Roman Fluted Vases. White terra-cotta. On Stair Balustrade.

103. 2 Roman Fluted Vases. White terra-cotta. On Stair Balustrade. From Scotland.

FLORAL ART GARDEN,

North Division.

104. 3 Reflecting Globes (red, white and blue) on Ornamented Iron Stands. From Paris.

105. Spatulated Greek Vase. White terra-cotta. Scotland.

106. Wicker-Basket Vase. Iron, on Pedestal.

107. Fluted Roman Vase. White terra-cotta.

108. Statue, "Hide and Seek. Whoop!" Terra-cotta. Rogers.

109. High Fluted Greek Vase. Terra-cotta. Scotland.

110. Spatulated do. do. do.

111. Statue, Flora. By Wittig. Zinc.

112. do. "Dhudeen-evus Euterpe."

113. High Fluted Greek Vase. Terra-cotta.

114. Wicker-Basket Vase. Iron.

115. Fluted Roman Vase. White terra-cotta.

116. 2 Seats, Imitation Tree Stumps. Red and white terra-cotta.

117. Chapel Fountain, Statue. Venus on the half shell after Finelli. Surrounded by 2 Greek Vine Vases, terra-cotta, and 2 Fruit Vases, white marble.

Mosaic Garden.

118. Wicker-Basket Flower Urn. White terra-cotta. From Scotland.

119. 2 Greek Fluted Vases. White terra-cotta, on Pedestals.

120. 1 Water Lilac Vase. White terra-cotta. Scotland.

121. 2 Florentine Vases. Black   do.   do.

122. 2 Greek Fluted Vases. White   do.   do.

123. Bust, Danaïde. By Rauch. White zinc. Surrounded by 4 Etruscan Vases, white terra-cotta, and 2 Florentine Vases, black zinc bronze, 2 Cellini Vases.

124. Reclining Elk. By Rauch. White zinc bronze.

125. Statue, Murmuring Waters. By Pradier. Black terra-cotta.

Lower Terrace Balustrade.

126. Antique Venus on the rail. Bust.

127. Etruscan Vase.

128. Bust. George Washington. Terra-cotta.

129. Etruscan Vase.

130. Bust, Sabrina. Terra-cotta. By B. Thorwaldsen.

131. Etruscan Vase.

132. Statue, Goddess of Triumph. Terra-cotta.

133. Etruscan Vase.

134. Gen. Lafayette. Terra-cotta.

135. Etruscan Vase.

136. Bust, Galileo. Terra-cotta.

137. do. B. Franklin. Terra-cotta.

138. Statue, Summer. Black do.

139. do. Autumn. do. do.

140. Bust, Ulysses (2d) S. Grant. White terra-cotta.

141. Statue, Cupid playing with Fish. do. do.

142. Etruscan Vase.

143. Bust, A. Lincoln. do. do.

144. Etruscan Vase.

145. Statue, Diana de Gabie. do. do. antique.

146. Etruscan Vase.

147. Bust, Venus de Milo. do. do. do.

148. Etruscan Vase.

149. Bust, Daniel Webster. do. do.

150. Etruscan Vase.

151. Statue, Psyche. White terra-cotta. B. Thorwaldsen.

Under Trellis Work.

152. Bust, Christoforo Colombo. White terra-cotta, on
Pedestal.

Aboretum Circle.

153. Fountain, Statues, Greek Slave. H. Powers.

Venus. B. Thorwaldsen.

153.   Fountain, Statues, Venus in the Bath.   Pradier.

Urania.   Antique, surmounted
by Tritons and Dolphins.

154.   Gnome Drinking-Fountain.   Bronze and granite.

155.   Statue, Santa Claus.   Colored wood.

156.   do.   Flora.   By Rauch.   Moulded clay.

157.   Frog Fountain.   "Home, Sweet Home — be it ever
so humble, there's no place like home," under an
umbrella in a shower.

158.   Boy riding on a Goat.   White zinc bronze.

159.   Girl   do.   do.   do.   do.

160.   Boston Fire Monument.   Four gigantic granite pil-
lars saved from the Boston fire, November 9, 1872.
Surmounted by Giovanni di Bologna's statue of
Mercury, the messenger of the Grecian gods.

First Department.

Norino Tower.

Odysseus (Ulysses).   Bronze, marble pedestal.

Leonardo da Vinci.   do.

Galileo.   do.

Richard Cœur de Lion.   do.

Philippe Auguste.   do.

Brennus.   Parian marble.

Bellona. Porcelain.

Pattas Athène. Porcelain.

Chinese Mandarin. Papier-maché. From Chinese Department, Centennial.

Chinese Lady. Papier-maché. From Chinese Department, Centennial.

Japanese Armor.

    do. War Dogs. Bronze.

1 Mediæval Armor. Iron and steel.

Gladiator Borghese. Bronze.

Idol, carved from roots in the Pacific Islands.

TIVOLI.

1 Billiard Table.

3 Tivoli   do.

1 Erratic Spinner, or the Devil among the Tailors.

1 Stereoscope.

Faust, Marguerite and Mephistopheles. Haute relief, Parian.

War. Haute relief, Parian.

Peace.   do.   do.

The Erl King. Haute relief, Parian.

Canova's Venus. Terra-cotta, on pedestal.

    do. Psyche.   do.   do.

Mary, Queen of Scots. Bronze.

Ceres. Antique medallion.

Pomona. do.   do.

Cinderella. By Cauer. Parian marble.

Heads of several famous persons, nodding to all visitors.

> The visitor, by inserting his head through the hole in a large card-board suspended at the southwest corner of the hall, will be surprised at finding himself portraited as drinking a mug of ale.

Cherubs carrying Globe, on marble pedestal. Antique.

Large Fish, from Japan.

Victory. Wittig. On Pedestal.

Medallion Vase. Florentine marble.

Ophelia, Canova. Parian marble.

> Please notice the curious portraying or allegorical hallucination of one afflicted with neuralgia.

Courtship in Sleepy Hollow. J. Rogers. Parian.

Rip Van Winkle and Snyder. On pedestal.

Diana de Versailles. Antique. Parian.

Thalia.   do.   do.

Head of Venus. Antique. On pedestal.

Silver Globe.

Canova's Psyche. On pedestal.

do.   Hebe.   do.

Edward the Confessor. On pedestal.

Harold.   do.

> Two ancient kings — but, like all mortals, made of clay.

Model of Church of Notre Dame in Montreal. Made of
wire, and intended for use as a bird-cage. Paris
Exhibition, 1867.

Dulcimer.

Harp.

The printer of this book returns this 85th page, end-
ing with the word " Harp," and requires twenty lines, —
no more, no less, as all before, and most all after, has been
electrotyped, — to fill out this page. The little "imp'
has repeatedly tied me down to lines, pressing my crayon
to limited minutes of time, in order not to stop his press.
It seems as though he was playing on this word " harp,"
probably " of a thousand strings," leaving me only one,
and that one binding me, brains and hand, under his
printing-press. The brain, forced, doesn't make forced-
meat, but it does *hash* one mentally; and whenever any
siding from the subject matter under consideration has
occurred, the reader will please credit it to pressing calls
to fill the printer's-press vacuum. The encroachment on
the Arcadium, which is devoted to such matters as interest
children, for the display of certain reminders of those who
were children one hundred years ago, is rendered necessary because the owner has no other suitable place to locate
the historic household articles used by those children of
the 17th and 18th centuries, now matured in the eternal life.

TEMPORARILY IN THE ARCADIUM

WILL BE FOUND

A LOT OF OLD-TIME RELICS,

Dating back to the year 1630,

Showing us how those lived who settled our rocky soil, and toiled in the 17th and 18th centuries, and picturing to our minds the advance of the present age in household art and science.

1. An ancient volume, entitled, " Commentariorvm de Regno Christi," by Philippo Nicolai. Printed by Johannes Spies, at Frankfort-on-the-Main, in 1597 (280 years old).

2. "Harmonia Evangelica." Frankfort-on-the-Main, 1622 (255 years old).

3. German volume, entitled, " A great collection for the religious. In which the belief of right and honesty in the life of a Christian and God's children, is eternal, majestic and glorious. Compiled by M. Martino Statio, Priest of St. John Dantzic, under the superintendence of Henry, John and Arndten Stern." Printed by John and Henry Stern, in Lunenburg, in 1652 (225 years old).

4. Gerard's "Ioannis Vossii de Theologia Gentiti et Physilogia Christiana." Amsterdam, 1663 (214 years old).

5. "Concordia pia et Unanimi confeufu repetita Confessio." Leipsic, 1685 (192 years old).

6. "Johannis Lasseria." Copenhagen and Leipsic, 1701 (176 years old).

7. Bichmann's "Hand Concordance." Leipsic, 1796 (81 years old).

8. Two Ottoman Frames —

Made from an English oak table, brought from England by Capt. Abram Brown, in the year 1630, only ten years after the landing of the Pilgrims at Plymouth. Capt. Abram settled with his companions, the Saltonstalls, in what is now Watertown, but was then by the Indians called by the not very classic name of Pigs-gusset. Benjamin Brown, grandson of Captain Abram Brown, was born February 27 A.D. 1681, prospected and erected his cabin, in 1702, on a high rocky eminence, in what is now Lincoln, but then was a part of Watertown. Here, in a very primitive way, lived "Deacon Ben," as he was called, with his eleven rugged children. The quaint old furniture and household ware used by "Deacon Ben" have passed from his generation down to his sons, and children's children, to the present time. Consequent upon the death of Miss Abigail H. Brown, without direct heirs, has resulted the sale, by auction, on August 7, 1877, of all the quaint collection, gathered and kept well in use in this old cabin home, which has now thirty-three rooms grafted on to it by the five generations of Browns who have succeeded to its ownership. The simple ways of these descendants, from Abram the captain (but worthy representative of Abra-

ham the Faithful and great sacrificer), has permitted the use of
the same old household furniture and house utensils since the
house was built in 1702. The innovations of fashion have not
reached this primitive hearth home. Descending with the descendants, the habit of old association has reserved the same corner for
the rag and button bag; the same nooks for fish-hooks, bullet-
moulds, &c.; the same shelf for the flint and tinder-box, though,
since the time of lucifer and friction matches, A.D. 1829, this shelf
has been otherwise used.

As we examine and hunt up the associations connected with
the articles bought by the owner of the Ridge Hill Farms, at this
sale of souvenirs of Capt. Abram Brown, we may well ask our-
selves if the advance of art and science, and the greater density of
population, has not deteriorated the nobler attributes of man, so far
as relates to honesty, truth and self-sacrifice. Are we of this age
of the same bold daring in doing our duty; of the same fearless
willingness to suffer for conscience' sake, or to work out any
unselfish aim in life? Is it not got to be plot and counterplot how
to manipulate or control the executive authority for the self-
advancement of the few at the expense of the many?

Is there not proof of this in the action of the city officials of this
present year, by their yielding to the importunate solicitation of
the residents in East Boston, known as Noddle's Island, who accepted their habitation, separated by the laws of Nature and of the
Great Controller, by a water division, from the other citizens of
Boston, and now wish those whom we find, from a careful scru-
tiny of the city records, number more than eleven twelfths of the
voters, and who pay more than thirty-nine fortieths of the city taxes,
to pay for *free* ferriage to this *now* beggars'-corner, in their fear
that the South Boston flats will be improved and their real estate
become " as dead as Chelsea " (WAS)? The reader of this " Guide
to Ridge Hill Farms " may think this a digression, but he will
find his mistake before " Finis " is reached. The reader should
reflect, when viewing these evidences of household life of the

seventeenth and eighteenth centuries, that we of the nineteenth, though living in the age of invention and the useful application of science in matters pertaining to our household, are liable, by having mechanical contrivances do our household work, to regard that class of the human species required to assist us in the "chores" of domestic life, as mere automatic machines, who are to be only "*pointed*" to their duties, supposing that they have been born and trained to a full knowledge of how properly to perform them. They forget that these human organizers (?) required for the domestic duties of every householder have, Topsy-like, only "*grown*" to their work, without any teaching, and therefore should not be regarded "as regular as clockwork" in other than *dis*-organizing the peace and comforts of the home.

The age is progressive. The Constitution, framed in 1780-81 for our Union of States, requires modification to hold good for us of the following centiade. The system of elective franchise, the influences warping executive administration, have changed as much as that of household economy since one hundred years ago, and we are required to carefully study the emergencies of our age, and regulate our laws and social life in conformity thereto.

The sparse population, and self-sacrificing honesty of the times that are gone, *gone,* properly permitted every one who paid his petty poll-tax, to have his birth-right privilege of voting. But the great increase of population has very essentially changed the relative dependence upon each other which existed in every small colony.

Under the existing system, those paying only two dollars annually, obtain the elective franchise, and by it — inasmuch as they compose four fifths of the voters — they really make the laws which are executed, at the expense of the remaining one fifth who pay forty-nine fiftieths of the entire taxes; in fact, very many improvements which may be outwardly whitewashed as of a public character, are more for the benefit of a few, and carried out at the expense of a very small proportion, possibly one tenth or less, of the citizens, and of those resident in such a section as to have no interest whatever in the so-called *public* improvement. Thus a very limited class of our citizens in Boston who take no part in paying the bills, have a four-fifths majority vote in making our laws and expenditures, and this is more or less true of the State and National Executive and expenditures.

We find that in 1877 the taxes in Boston are assessed on a total valuation, real and personal, of $686,802,100, which, at the rate of $13.10 on the thousand dollars of valuation, sums up the total warrant to $8,754,214, of which eighty-six thousand and seven, paying two dollars each, is only $172,014, or less that one fiftieth; and yet those representing this small fraction, control the executive and the expenditures of the city, and consequently the pockets of those who pay more than forty-nine fiftieths of the city taxes. Over seventy-eight per cent of the voters in Boston in A.D. 1874, were assessed on polls only. One hundred years ago the expenditures of the city were very small. The warrant for the years previous to 1803 are difficult to trace, by reason of the records having been destroyed by fire. That of 1803 shows the entire warrant of the town of Boston to be $125,825; the number of tax bills, *i.e.*, number of those assessed, were 4483, and 1225 bills abated in whole or in part. Thus there was a more equal and average payment of taxes than in these times, when the expenditures are largely to benefit a class, or section of, rather than the total of the citizens. The statute as originally enacted, and never changed, provided that one sixth of the warrant should be assessed on polls, but the polls were not ever to exceed two dollars; thus the first part of the law became inoperative, and now the proportion, in place of being one sixth, is only one fiftieth. The *double* tax on mortgages, which is so oppressive to the poor, should be rescinded, and the poll-tax should be raised to ten dollars. It would then only net less than one tenth of the total warrant. But if *pro rata* with the requirements to cover appropriations each year, it would be more equitable, and would check the at present tendency to "jobs" or improper and unnecessary expenditures, and lay the foundation for a true civil service reform, which would tolerate, from interested motives, only such in official positions as were suitable for, and worthy of the place. This is quite different from the present system, wherein those who have the majority of the election, and through it the appointing power, merely make drafts upon the pockets of those who pay forty-nine fiftieths of the taxes, in order to allow lazy John, inefficient Jim, or "treating" George to live in clover and honey. Can we not regulate temperance reform by licensing the sale of ardent spirits in such a sum as is sufficient to cover the annual expenditures for police, criminal courts and correctionary institutions, and collecting *pro rata* of the remaining taxes required, per capita on the polls, and on such real or personal property as it may be deemed policy to assess?

Cannot the national revenue be collected per capita on the polls, and on specific duties on imports on those articles classed as luxuries, and thus make voters pecuniarily interested in civil-service reform, and honest importers protected from their dishonorable competitors, who cheat the customs, bribe officials, and generally demoralize the community?

Should not international expositions tend to freedom of thought, reciprocity of trade. international protection for the individual of each and every nation from piracy, murder, forgery, theft, and crime of every character? Can this result be reached while we discriminate in favor of certain products and special nations? Can the co-association of citizens as a Friday Reform Club help about a change from the old-rut routine, and place us on a basis more in conformity to that in which our age differs from that which was one hundred years ago?

Are not these thoughts rationally the legitimate uprisings from viewing these old-time relics, which at once associate the men, the manner of life, and the requisites of the government service of that age in comparison to that in this second centiade of our national existence?

How much of the old furniture and dinner ware could be shown with as few " chips," from the china, and broken parts of the utensils and furniture, if other than the " gude housewife " and her home domestic daughters had washed, scrubbed and had the care of it! "Rough and ready," has been the motto. " Rough and honest," should not be as fossils. Reader, please do not be a mere automatic-machine thinker as you examine these old-time relics, but reflect upon that which kept these articles in such good condition, and that which is required, in the present time, to conform to the requirements of our age.

Many articles have no initials or dates designating their age, and are doubtless much older than the date herein given, back to which time initials, corroborated by descriptive wills, deeds and documentary evidence, reliably place them.

9.   Square table with out-pointed toed legs.   1735.
     Top restored with a new one, one hundred years ago.

10.   Silver knee-buckles.   1740.

11.   Wardrobe or portable closet.   1740.

A large portion of the articles following are known to have been in use by the family of Timothy Brown, 2d, who was born A.D. 1750, and married Hannah Lee, of Concord, in 1772.   Some of them were her marriage portion: —

12.   Oak Frame Loom, with harness-cards and shuttles for
       hand-weaving.   On this was made the cloth for all
       the family garments.

13.   Flax Reel, Hatchell and Wheel for spinning linen
       thread.

14.   Large Wheel for spinning woollen yarn.

15.   Wheel for winding the bobbins.

16. Reel Swift, on old log pedestal.

17. 1 Upright-bar, high-back, rush-bottom chair.

18. 9 Cross-bar, high-back, rush-bottom chairs.

19. 4 Parlor chairs, moquetry.

20. Bed Warming-pan. Long iron handle.

21. Looking-glass.

22. Cherry Desk. Secret Drawers.

23. Round two-leaf Table.

24. Pine Cradle. that has rocked many a " lullaby-baby " to sleep.

25. Old Saddle.

26. Snow-shoes.

27. Old Razors, that have got well rested, and thus show a keen, sharp edge.

28. Old Button-bag and contents, including buttons used during the commencement of the present century.

29. Butter Scales made entirely of wood.

30. Eight Pewter Dinner Plates and two Platters, very heavy, marked " H. L."

31. Three Pewter Porringers, " H. L.," one Pewter Cup, one Pitcher, two Salt Cellars and two Vegetable Basins.

32. Blue and white Cup and Saucer, Swan and Daisy pattern, very old.

33. 3 White China Dinner Platters, with blue edge; China Pepper-box and Mustard Cruet.

34. Set of Dinner Knives, including Carvers and Bone Cleavers; some of which are worn to within two inches of the handle, and two thirds of the original width of the blade ground away by sharpening.

35. Set of "Company Knives," the handles made from the bones of animals.

36. 3 Iron Candlesticks, with hooks to hang them on the back of a chair.

37. 2 Brass Andirons, the iron rests quite burnt through.

38. Baby Chair, used, probably, by all the Brown babies.
     Its pink covering induces all babies "to take to it" immediately.

All of the above are well authenticated as having been used by Hannah (*née* Lee) Brown, who was married in 1772.

Of the following articles, some are nearer the commencement of the 19th century, and others again are of ante-bellum (1775) times : —

39. The "Gore" Crib.

> This was presented to one of the Brown family, perhaps as a marriage gift, by Christopher Gore, who was born in England in A.D. 1758, was Governor of Massachusetts in 1809-1810, and in whose office Daniel Webster studied law, and by whose advice Webster declined the position offered to him of clerk of the Court of Common Pleas of New Hampshire, immediately after his admission to the bar.

40. Umbrella.

The cloth covering showing that it either never had *any color*, or if it had, that it was *not a fast color*. Its frame is of whale-bone, stayed by double wires. The stick and handle is of dark wood, and altogether its general appearance would convey the impression that it had been carefully preserved since its use at the commencement of the rain when Shem, Ham and Japhet, with their father Noah, entered the Ark.

Unhappily, the fact that umbrellas were not generally used until A.D. 1778, disturbs the poetry of this antique umbrella.

41. Grain, Snow and Cider-apple Shovels.

Made with a jack-knife by Isaac Brown, who was born in 1680, and in his boyhood days was a great whittler. They average twelve by sixteen inches at the shovel part, and have handles vary-ing from four to five feet in length, each whittled by the pocket-knife from one piece of lumber. It seems like chopping down a large tree and whittling the trunk into a tea-spoon.

42. 8 old Jack-knives and 3 loose pocket-knife blades.

43. Five Cider-apple Baskets,

Also made by Isaac Brown; one of them, being nearly four feet in diameter, holds eight bushels, and would be just the thing as a floral tribute, filled with one entire hot-house of flowers, to Miss Clara Louise Kellogg, Miss Adelaide Phillips (the "pretty, pretty Polly Hopkins" of our boyhood associations), or other sweet native songstress.

44. Dinner and Tea Set of Blue Crockery.

These were known to be in use about the commencement of the nineteenth century. They are remarkably free from "chipping."

45. Wine Glasses.

Were in use by the same Brown family as used the No. 44 Blue Crockery. But these glasses are supposed to be over one hundred years old; and he that interpreted the expression, " Wine is better in old bottles," to mean old glass, would probably get his head turned if he imbibed from these ancestral glasses.

46.   Padlocks.

One of them very quaint, — reminding one of Bluebeard and the legend age.

47.   *Chapeau*, marked on a metal tablet " A. H. A. [Ancient and Honorable Artillery] A.D. 1638."

By some this might possibly be regarded as made at that date, and to have been worn by Captain Keayne, one of the founders of this antique company, who by his dying bequest left it five sterling pounds and one new-milch cow, were it not that the imprint on the inside reads " Bent & Bush, Boston;" and most of us well know that this Bush is not so old or Bent with age as to date away back to A.D. 1638.

48.   Pair of Rubbers,

Sold in 1824 by John Rogers, not he that was burnt at his stake, but he that has been cornered, ever so many years, at the junction of Tremont St. and Pemberton Square, where old Gardner Green's slippery-elm trees grew, to the delight of slippery school-boys.

These Rubbers or Elastic Treaders seem to have been made in a very primitive fashion, apparently after a similar manner that the Irishman described the making of cannon; namely, taking a *hole* somewhat resembling the foot of Jeremy Drake, for forty-two years the revered cashier of the Freemans National Bank, for whom they were intended, and covering it (the hole) with a very irregular layer of crude gum rubber, one half inch in thickness. Contrast this old-time elastic foot-dressing of 1824 with that of Rogers' or H. H. Tuttle's present style of ladies' wear, which are found by the side of it, and tell us if you do not think that it is time to correct the old proverb which reads " *Le style c'est l'homme*," so as to read "*Le style c'est la femme*."

49. Military Coat and Chapeau,

> Worn by Major-General   in the war of 1812.

50. The Bedstead on which slept General Lafayette at the residence of his Excellency, Governor Eustis, in Savin Hill, Dorchester, in 1824.

During the last year of tae administration of President Munroe an invitation had been extended by our General Government to the Marquis de Lafayette, to visit the United States as the guest of the nation. He accepted the invitation, and arrived in New York on Sunday, August 15, 1824, with his son George Washington Lafayette.

From the Massachusetts "Centinel," and a communication from General W. H. Sumner, of Jamaica Plain, published, in 1859, in the Historical Register, we clip this history concerning

51. The Table used at the Dinner given by Governor Eustis in honor of General Lafayette, on Friday, August 27, 1824 :   .

" His Excellency Governor Eustis had directed two of his aides, with conveyances, to be at the line of the Commonwealth, in Pawtucket, to await the arrival of Lafayette, who reached there at six P.M., Monday, August 23d, and rode all night, being received by the villages *en route* with greetings of ladies and citizens and bonfires ; in Dedham, by a general illumination of the houses ; in Roxbury, by salvos of artillery ; and escorted by numerous citizens he reached the mansion of his Excellency Governor Eustis, in Dorchester, at two o'clock Tuesday morning, thus redeeming his pledge that he would be in the vicinity of Boston on Monday."

General Sumner thus writes : " The Governor gave an elegant breakfast, and then the troops, which were ordered for the escort, proceeded with him to Boston. On reaching the State House the

Governor then welcomed Lafayette in a formal manner, in the name of the Commonwealth, the ceremony taking place in the Council Chamber."

"The following day being Commencement at Cambridge, Lafayette was the honored guest of the University. His seat upon the platform in the meeting-house, where the usual ceremonies of the occasion were performed, was on the right hand of the Governor. On the opposite part of the platform, where I had my seat, the Governor beckoned to me, and on approaching him, intervening the parts, he addressed me rapidly: 'I wish to speak to you, Gen. Sumner, in your capacity as Quartermaster General, or as Commissary General, as I might more properly express it, to ask you if you can get me a dinner at my house to-morrow, in honor of this gentleman and thirty or forty others whom I intend to invite, many of whom are here?' I replied that I had not had much practice in providing dinners, *in my capacity of Quartermaster General*, and that the powers of Commissary General were not confided to me. Gov. Eustis said, 'If so, I know you have had great experience in getting dinners at home.' I said that I would, individually, do everything that I could to accomplish his wishes. I would state to him, however, for his consideration, that all the provisions and delicacies of the market had been selected for the entertainment at Cambridge that day, and that all the public servants who could be hired, were also at Cambridge, and it would be as difficult to collect his guests on the next day as it would be to get provisions or servants for the entertainment. But, I said, 'If you will postpone it one day, I will take upon myself the responsibility that it shall be done, although I do not know, at the present time, whom I shall employ to do it.' The Governor said, 'I see it is impossible, as you suggest, to have it to-morrow; but I will ask him for Friday, upon the assurance you have given, for I know of no one else that I can call upon to assist me.'

"Although it was not a part of my public duty to provide an enter

tainment for his company at his private mansion, I daresay the
Governor thought my duty would be embraced in the order which
he had given me.

"As this was the first time he had called upon me to do anything
but office business, and especially as he had recently come into
power, succeeding Gov. Brooks, by the election of the democratic
party, in opposition to that under which I held my office, I did not
think it worth while to be very particular. I therefore went to
work, with more zeal perhaps than I should have done if the enter
tainment had been given by the Governor's predecessor, or by any
one else of the same party in politics. 'Well,' said the Governor,
'I must tell you another thing, sir, and that is, that I do not wish
to give Mrs. Eustis any trouble except that which results from the
use of the house. They may have my kitchen and my parlors and
my chairs and tables; but as to having my knives and forks, and
plates and dishes, they shall not have one of them. My decanters
I will fill with wine and other suitable liquors, which shall be de-
livered to the man who prepares the dinner, in proper order to
place upon the table. Now, do you think you can get any person
to undertake it on those terms? If so, I will ask Lafayette to
dine with me on that day, as he is soon to leave this place.' I said
'that it was something of an undertaking to do it so suddenly,
and on those terms, and that I knew of but one man who could accomplish it, and that I would go to see him that afternoon and get
him to do it, or let him know that evening, if he would delay
giving his invitation to the principal guest for a few hours.'

"I went to Col. Hamilton of the Exchange Coffee House, an ex-
cellent, cool-headed and systematic caterer, upon any sudden
emergency, in his own house, whose ability I had often witnessed
in giving some of the most splendid entertainments that Boston,
at that time, exhibited. Hamilton acceded to my request, and
agreed to undertake it, as, he said, 'that for a guest to whom the
nation owes so much, every person ought to do the best he can.
Though it would seem to many almost impossible to accomplish

this, you may rest assured, Gen. Sumner, that it shall be done as well as I can do it.' I replied, 'You had better go out to the Governor's, and see how he wishes his tables laid, and what you will need, before you do anything else.' He did so, and satisfied the Governor that it should be all accomplished in the manner he desired, without any trouble to Mrs. Eustis.

"At the dinner the plates were placed on the outside of a horse-shoe table, in the hall, leaving the inside open for the attendance of the servants and the change of dishes. There were between thirty and forty guests, the Governor taking his position at the head of the table, with Lafayette on his right, Gen. Dearborn on his left, the late Gov. Brooks second on the right, the Lieutenant-Governor and Council, the Governor's Military Staff and other guests, which are not now recollected, seated on each side."

52. The Coach owned by Governor Eustis,

And in which, on the right side, on the rear seat, rode General Lafayette, on Tuesday, August 24, 1824, when officially received in procession by the Executive of the Commonwealth, and the Executive of the City of Boston, and with great ovations by the masses of citizens. It is recorded of Governor Eustis "that before his inauguration he rode only in an open wagon with one horse, which was familiarly known as his electioneering wagon, it was so often seen during the canvass at the gates of his political friends. After his inauguration he kept a very handsome coach. Governor Brooks, his predecessor in office, never owned a four-wheeled carriage, but always drove with a single horse and chaise."

These Eustis-Lafayette souvenirs were purchased for Ridge Hill Farms from Fred. Hassam, of Dorchester, who bought them at the sale of the Eustis estate and effects, in the year A.D. 1864.

We must leave to the imagination of the visitor many articles which we cannot enumerate herein.

The " sweetness," whatever there may be of it in this

Guide, is now long drawn out. The patience of the reader, although endowed with a large allotment from old Biblical Job (the supposed inventor of the Job wagon), has been, probably, quite exhausted. We have given that important, none-other-such rare-ripe scholar, the book critic, a big capital or Archimedian lever, with which, petard-like, to hoist us so far into the heavens above, and then drop us down, down into the region below, as to save you, reader, from another similar infliction to this Guide, the first pages of which went to press with a size selected for a ten to fifteen page pamphlet, which we are likely now to string out to near one hundred and thirty, largely because the printer's " devil " has so continuously pressed us " for copy," and our obstinate wish to " give him his dues."

We wish to give you a bit of rest, and an opportunity to commune with that one whom you think the most of in all this world, and whom you so often lead astray, — YOUR- SELF; we wish to tickle your individual glory, incite your heart to controlling you to active co-operation and co-association in the important work which is on before, and toward which this is the Guide, as will be enumerated in part three joined hereto.

The hand that obeys the will of the heart has myste- riously lead us to dive deep into the statistics of history, and controlled our plumbago hieroglyphics (the frequent calls of the printer's "devil-apprentice" have led us to lay aside the porcupine quill) toward that work of Social Science, the Aim of Life, which we expected would be reached at a subsequent step. We do not *beg* you to hear us yet awhile and favorably consider our plea. We only say, if you do not care further to read this, then don't. Read, if you read, act, if you act, of your own free will. Let your heart be its own mentor. Do that which your heart dictates, freely, and do not wait for solicitation. If you take no interest, have no sympathy, in that to which this Guide — and the entire Ridge Hill Farms estate — portends, then say so, and oppose it with all your might and main; — and by so doing, you may incite to activity those showing a lukewarm interest, and be of more service than if you took out your pocket-book and helped lay the corner-stone.   FINIS.

Yours, at service,

PLUMBAGO CRAYON.

NOTE.

Before enchaining your mind by that which follows in the third part, we wish to give proper credit, first, to Antonio Passucci, a young Italian, now having his studio at 7 Pemberton Square, Boston, for the large painting showing the State House, and the portraits of the prominent statesmen of our Massachusetts Bay Colony in the

17th and 18th centuries, the panel paintings and the niche statuary of the Boat-house, and for the panel cartoons done by him at the Piggery.

Second, to W. L. Williams, artist, still engaged at Ridge Hill Farms, who painted Lief Ericson (in less than ten hours' work), and that of the large cartoon seen on the roof of the black and gold stable, portraying the Horses of the Sun and the attendant Horen. By the aid of the Camera and lime-light this subject was magnified, from a five-inch square negative, to cover a canvas measuring 16x34 feet; this the artist outsketched with charcoal crayons, in thirty-five minutes, and with a rapidity of hand and brain quite deserving of this special commendation, finished the relievo painting in less than *forty hours'* actual work. He is now engaged on the "Union of Hopes and Union of Hearts," for the Union Monument Headquarters. Those qualities required by the host to execute numerous projected illuminations at fêtes or surprises for the grounds, and give finishing brush-touches to ornamental works, buildings, &c., have been found in the artist Williams, and with him, and the general superintendent, Richard Greaves, has the host communed when planning the work seen accomplished at Ridge Hill Farms. Of the superintendent nothing need be said, inasmuch as "by his deeds shall ye know him." The garden speaks, as no words can, of the skill and taste of the man. Earnest, zealous, and with his whole heart engaged many, *many*, MANY consecutive nights, continued far into the morning hours, has he, with matches and candles, walked over the grounds with the owner, building castles in the air, removing obstacles to progress, projecting ornamental water-works, fountains, artificial ponds and lakes, and planning wonders underground.

The architect who has most assisted the host at Ridge Hill Farms is George F. Meacham, of Boston ; not bound, as many architects are, to variations of only one school of study; originating with a free hand, conforming to the projector's views, yet finishing and harmonizing with a classic touch, — to him is entitled the credit of displaying the master-hand in all such structures as may be admired at Ridge Hill Farms, while those not pleasing, and where the " classic touch " is out of sight, may be credited to — somebody else.

ERRORS AND OMISSIONS.

Seven of those who, by special permission, were allowed to pass through the grapery on August 25, were reported as having stolen Hamburg grapes. The lady in black, about fifty years of age, who divided her spoils just outside, did not give her son a very moral maternal lesson

Lovers of others' fruits are cautioned against man and woman traps, shower-baths, swarms of hornets, wasps and bees, so arranged that the least touch of a grape-stem may revolve the flapper, tumble the fluids, or electrify the varmints, and get the biter bit.

Those who used the Norino Tower as a spittoon on August 29, must remember that those who expectorate in private houses, cannot expect-to-rate as gentlemen.

A fair sample of this class is that of a party of seven who came to the Registry Office on Tuesday, September 4, the spokesman saying, " We wish to go everywhere and see everything on this place; will you tell us where to go?" The lady in charge described, in detail, the places of interest, and added, " You will sign your names on the register, and then you can go everywhere on the grounds, in the hot-houses, amimal houses, &c.; but if you wish to go into the Tower, Arcadium, Grotto and Camera, you will have to pay twenty-five cents each for the service employed." — " It is an imposition — a regular humbug — to get us out here and charge us this. Mr. Baker is feathering his pockets nicely." — " Mr. Baker does not get one cent of it, any more than you do, sir; if there be anything over the sum necessary to pay the wage of twenty persons, employed exclusively, by reason of permitting visitors to the grounds and buildings, it is to be given to a Boston charity;

if you came on the regular visiting days, Wednesdays or
Saturdays, the service-fee would be only ten cents. To
protect himself from being swarmed with visitors every
day, and in order to cover the expense of keeping those
employed on the off days, the fee was set at twenty-five
cents for the off days." — " All stuff and nonsense, madam :
I know better than that; I don't believe a word of it. It is
all a catch and a lie. The charity is all pop-in-cock; and
Mr. Baker puts it all in his pocket." — " This is *not* a public garden, sir, where any one who pays can come. It is
not *advertised* as you say, sir. It is a private estate, kept
up at a great expense, very much greater expense by
reason of the thefts, carelessness and lawlessness of the
visitors whom he permits freely to visit the grounds, if
they merely register their names. The fees to enter the
buildings may cover for the service, but most certainly do
not cover for the thefts, indiscretions and breakage, of visitors. If you object to the fee, register your name, sir, and
you can go anywhere on the grounds except on the avenue
immediately in front of the owner's front door."—" Well,
I am here, and I don't mean to come again, so I must, I
suppose. submit to the extortion — here's your pay; " and
he ostentatiously displayed a large roll of bills, the smallest
of which was found to be of the denomination of ten dollars; which, as Miss Ward could not change at that hour

of the morning, one of the ladies accompanying him finally presented a five dollar greenback.

This man was about fifty-five years of age, semi-gray hair, and keeps a hotel in Boston, the printed cards of which, about three weeks previous to this, Sept. 4th inst., were found strewn on the ground on the Arboretum Knoll, with a large lot of garbage from some picnic baskets, consisting of rinds of watermelons, pastry and old meat bones, the which are not ornamental to dressed grounds. Such deposits, and his insinuating language at the Registry Office, try the patience of the owner and those assisting him, and suggest the thought to one and all, that it would be pleasing to have him keep away and leave his old bones in some other place.

Many strangers, on being requested to register their names, say, "How absurd!" "What foolishness!" "What does the old fool want us to sign our names for!" These left-handed compliments to the owner and employés are not rare and exceptional, but frequent, and so prominent and annoying as to severely test the patience of a saint, though he may have charity oozing from every one of the pores in each square inch of the mortal frame.

Those who *preach* about the soft answer subduing this tainted talk, are here wanted to *practise* that which they preach, and heap coals of fire on the heads of those "Innocents Abroad," who, doubtless, make a large display of thin-skinned courtesy and politeness when in their homes.

Miss Harriot Ward, who has the charge of the Register Book, and acts as an animated guide, is compelled to keep her tongue in perpetual motion answering funny questions, and is a regular American Nightingale (sister to Florence) in her opportunities to dispense from the medicine chest, indicate a quiet nook for rest to some fatigued and aged lady, or for some fond mother to put her baby to sleep. The sweet spices of her life are diversified and solaced with the oily talk of some, and the sharp, sour vinegar froth of others, fitting her to conquer, by faith and patience, while contending with these insect torments, quiet rest in the Registry Office above. To which, however, we hope she will not go at present, even if she is over forty, but remain in charge of this Registry here below, giving practical lessons in courtesy and gentle bearing, even towards those who are forgetful of all other than their own selfish wants.

The indiscretions for the month of August have been numerous and annoying. The devices to avoid paying the service-fee have been frequent. The reported penuriousness of the host in requiring the service-fee of those who visit the Ridge Hill Farms, and for allowing his children to sell peacock feathers, have been frequent and amusing. Such lack of consideration expressed by acts and words show the character of some of our American "people;" and those having art galleries, or art arboretums which they are benevolently inclined to allow strangers to visit, have been constrained, by similar discourtesies and abusive acts, to close their doors to all. Any one wishing to study character can find it well diversified by passing any Wednesday or Saturday at the Registry Office, in the Grotto, or about the grounds at Ridge Hill Farms. Newspaper scribblers can fill a column any day with the peculiarities of peculiar people.

ADDITIONS.

Reached Ridge Hill Farms September 3, two Java deer from Angers. These are about two years old, full growth, and yet are not larger than a medium-sized cat. This class are the cunningest little deers in the world. *Deer Tommie* died on September 4, and *Little Deer Jennie* needs your deer sympathy.

September 9th, arrived safely the two Seneca bears hereinbefore described.

Which description, on being read from printer's proof to Josiah Quincy, he corroborates the supposition concerning Florida having been the Garden of Eden, by the statement that other parts of our nation have some indications of antique visitors and settlers, inasmuch as the Potomac River is evidently from the Greek word *potamos*, meaning a river; and the Piscataqua River from the words *pisces et aqua;* thus giving us some ground to think that the Greek and Latin races visited our shores in by-gone ages and left the mounds and pottery which so disturb our archæologists,—unless it was by the children of Israel, who by some are supposed to have had the honor, long before Christopher Columbus, of having visited our shores, and deserted it by reason of the porcineograph outlines of these United States which they prophetically foresaw (see p. 131) or of some fatal disease which destroyed the settlers and led them ever after to eschew the *porcus* family and the country which resembled it.

The only weak part in this chain of evidence is the fact that it is not recorded that the Jews spoke Latin or Greek, although they, of course, spoke their own language, — Hebrew.

But as our venerable friend tells us of this derivation of the Potomac River, and as the Quincys have ever been prominent in good works, particularly in establishing the Quincy or Faneuil Hall Market, we accept his verification that the ancient Grecians came here, or else sent their language here, — which accounts (through the Quincy Market) for the name of "Modern Athens," because our citizens literally live in Grease, under the present system (?) of cookery.

The Charity Reservation

Of land on the 7th or Charity day of the Fraternal Welcome Fête (July 14th, 1876), is bounded by Charles River on the south and west, and by Charles River Street on the north. It encloses 350 acres, some of it in plateaux, by the river side, and again, on the high land, well suited for cultivation; while other parts are diversified by hills and knolls, cold springs and pine-tree groves.

Here is an *Artificial Fish-Pond* covering five acres, stocked two years ago with 30,000 trout spawn, and this spring with 2000 small-fry California salmon. Near by is the ornamental Wood Tower, 90 feet in height, for the Eclipse Windmill, which is thirty feet in diameter. This mill, with average wind, has about six-horse power, and lifts a five-inch column of water from the cold spring (48 degrees Fahrenheit) up to, and fills, in from four to five hours, the Reservoir, holding 50,000 gallons, on the Water Tower.

When all the fountains are continued in full play for a length of time the No. 14 Blake Steam Pump can fill this reservoir in three hours.

Southwest of the Artificial Fish-Pond, and near the Charles River, is the *Riverside Herd-Barn*, which in 1871 formed one of the cluster of farm buildings near the present site of the Chilian Pavilion. It was moved, full of hay, over three fourths of a mile, and placed here. It can accommodate, in its basement and on the first floor, fifty cows. Those here found at the evening milking hour consist of the Ayrshire, Brittany and Jersey stock. The most interesting of the latter breed are the two mouse-colored cows found on the north side in the fourth and fifth stalls from the east end.

One of them is called the "*Belle of Wellesley*," and was so named by the guests attending the fête on July 4, 1870, called the "Heifer-Calf Party;" each one invited having been requested to offer, in prose or rhyme, a name for the Jersey heifer, whose pedigree was specified.

A committee of three was chosen, consisting of Rev. Edward Everett Hale and Franklin W. Smith, of Boston, and Judge James W. Austin, of the Sandwich Islands, who selected eleven names from those submitted, and these were put to vote until the assemblage made choice of "*The Belle of Wellesley*," and the programme of the christening followed. The other cow was named in a similar fashion on July 4, 1871, at the fête specified as *" The Eddie and Walter and Belle of Wellesley's daughter party."

---

* The names of the two children of the proprietor.

The name selected was "*The Maid of the Mist.*" These two cows have been exceptionally attractive on many fête days, yielding, apparently, an *unlimited* quantity of milk, which, on being tasted by the guests, was found to be very strongly tinctured with the " plated spoon," or Old Medford, giving rise to many surmises as to these cows having browsed on rum-cherry foliage. The milker was carefully scrutinized, but no trick was discovered, the guest being allowed to take the teat in hand and taste his own milking. The phenomenon is thus accounted for: The fifth teat was of rubber, painted like the four others, and attached with gluten to the cow; connected with it was a very small rubber tube glutinized to the hind leg and colored to harmonize; thence it followed the woodwork, painted to match, to the hayloft, and there connected with a receptacle of warm milk punch.

South of this Herd-barn is the *Corner-Stone Piggery*, so named because the laying of the corner stone, on June 19, 1875, was the occasion of a frolic given in honor of the 5th Maryland National Guard and representatives of the Washington Light Infantry of Charleston, S.C., of the Light Artillery Blues of Norfolk, and of the Knights Templars of Richmond, Va., who were visiting Boston as participants in the Bunker Hill Centennial.

The host received his guests in a Marquee Pavilion

on the Conservatory Lawn near his residence. They then marched in procession or were conveyed in picnic wagons to the site of the new piggery. Prominent guests were seated on the platform there erected, and the others gathered on the side of *Charity Hill.* The Rev. Minot J. Savage, of Boston, opened the proceedings by prayer that from this frolic good might come; that men as they received pleasure should be mindful of extending it to those, daily met, overburdened with the cares and ills of life.

The Governor, William Gaston, followed, welcoming the guests from the South to the farm districts of Massachusetts. Curtis Guild, representing the city authorities, apologized for the absence of the Mayor in such a fashion as elicited roars of laughter from the three thousand guests assembled on the hillside.

Col. Andrews, of South Carolina, responded for the Southern guests in such choice language as won for him the admiration of all the ladies present. The host then improvised a part which was as much a surprise to the Marshals as to every one else, excepting Col. Jenkins, the Commander of the Maryland 5th Regiment, to whom he communicated his thought, and finding that the joke was heartily endorsed, he addressed Col. Jenkins, saying that he found his Regiment lacking in only one particular, that of not having any adopted " Daughter of the Regi-

ment," as had many European military organizations.
Therefore the host proposed to offer the Maryland 5th *une
fille du regiment* — would the Regiment adopt her? The
responsive " *Aye* " was strong and unanimous, and was
only drowned by the cheers and roars of laughter which
followed the host's taking from a large basket, which was
just then brought to him, a small white pig, and presenting
it with all due formality to Col. Jenkins, who responded,
holding with his left hand the little infant to his heart,
while the right hand moved in harmony to his felicitous
speech, which continued the laughter. As he was about
to return to his seat the host again addressed him, saying
that there had been a mistake made by his farm errand
boy sent to get the pig, who had been directed to bring a
Berkshire, which was of stock that had been imported
direct to Ridge Hill Farms from the Queen of England's
farm at Windsor, — thinking it appropriate, in this Centennial year, to symbolize the good feeling then existing
between Old England, from whom we cut the apron strings
one hundred years ago, and Massachusetts, Maryland and
the South, with the latter having had more recently some
misunderstanding. But now, as in all other cases, the
white had got ahead of the black species, yet the host
tendered the Berkshire, of another sex, to keep the Chester company. At this offering of the black pig there

were loud cheers for "The Twins." The continuance of this history of the miscegenation twins may be better described by here copying the following letter from the host, and the account from the Baltimore newspapers of what followed : —

RIDGE HILL FARMS,

WELLESLEY, Mass., June 29, 1875.

Col. J. STRICKER JENKINS,

*Fifth Regiment Maryland National Guard, Balti-
more, Md.*

My dear Sir, — The daughter of your regiment, or the younger of the two Centennial pigs presented to you at the laying of the corner-stone of the new piggery at Ridge Hill Farms, Wellesley, is yet only a sucking pig from a litter of June 6, and I have therefore delayed forwarding it. I intend to send her by Adams & Co.'s Express, Friday evening, July 2.

These two Centennial pigs — the white Chester (the daughter of your regiment), born in Massachusetts, and her black Berkshire cousin, of dam born at the Queen of England's farm at Windsor — arriving in Baltimore on the Fourth of July, may well typify the olive-branch and good-cheer bond *now* existing between Great Britain, Maryland and the good old Commonwealth of Massachusetts.

These porcine souvenirs of your visit to Ridge Hill
Farms will go forward in a wire cage. I had this cage
arranged with four arms, so that porters could bear it on
their shoulders from the Baltimore depot to your armory,
in company with three of my fête marshals, whom I had
delegated to convey and present to your regiment a *banner* to souvernize its participation at the June 19 fête; but
the superlative warmth of your complimentary newspaper
reports, &c., towards Bostonians has so frightened me that
I do not dare let any of my friends make an attempt to go
through Baltimore. If your kind-hearted distemper toward Bostonians is contagious, I fear your Adjutant General
will order out, as escort to these pigs, on the Fourth
of July celebration not only the Fifth Regiment, but all
the other regiments of your State, and also invite the co-
operation of those of all the other Southern States. I
therefore send as a personal escort to the *fille du regiment*,
one who is proof against all heat, be it of your kind hearts
or of the present season; viz., one of the representatives
of the Devil's Den at Ridge Hill Farms. As I send, however, only the shell, you will have to find one from your
own ranks to *animate* the devil. As the disturbed spirit
who roams around the shell of our mother earth seeks most
to bend the twig of childhood to formulate the rebellious
man, I also send the shell of one of those *babies* found in

the woods on June 19, into which you can place the biggest "baby" of your command, and on his and the devil's shoulders convey the daughter of the regiment and her cousin from the depot to your armory.

Thanking you for giving me the opportunity to receive your regiment at my farms, regretting that some of my good intentions, by reason of the storm, came to naught, I am, my dear sir, with three strings of distinguished consideration, a kernel (by brevet) of your honored regiment.   W. E. BAKER.

N.B. — At a suitable time, when you have had time to cool from your, at present, nine-days' warmth towards Bostonians, I shall take the opportunity to send you by the hands of a few lady and gentlemen friends the banner, &c., for your command.   W. E. B."

The proceedings at Baltimore are reported as follows in the Baltimore " News : " —

" As was predicted, yesterday was a jolly Fourth of July. The people were aroused at early dawn of day by the ringing of ' Big Sam,' a patriotic treat that no other city in the Union enjoyed. The arrival of the pigs from the Ridge Hill Farms was the grand event of the day. The Hub porkers reached the city early in the forenoon, and were kept in charge by David Boswell, 61 Granby Street, until the escort made its appearance. A 'News' reporter, having spent the day in reading the story of Washington and his little hatchet, as laid down in the order of the day by his superior officers, sallied forth to interview the porkers.

DESCRIPTION OF THE PIGS.

The little pig 'Loney,' he found to be a delicate blonde, weighing about seven pounds. Mr. Boswell was kind enough to drive his wagon behind the Point Market, to allow the enthusiastic in the crowd an opportunity to greet the stranger. 'Pontier,' the big pig, was dark-complexioned, the hair being mixed with gray. 'Pontier,' it was learned, devoured more soft crabs, fried oysters, spring chickens, Mary's little lambs, &c., than any other pig during the laying of the corner stone of Mr. Baker's new pig-stye, and yet it squeaked 'Let us have peas.' This, no doubt, accounts for the difference in the weight of 'Pontier' and 'Loney,' who don't like such things. At five o'clock the Fifth Regiment, in disguise, called for the pork. The escort was headed by a band of music, the notes of which have seldom, if ever, been surpassed. G. H. Spilker, Jr., was marshal of police, and wore the uniform of the man who first invented that valuable institution. Big Chief, T. J. Owens, furnished tobacco to the tribe, who delighted in the abundance of native product. The Modocs, headed by 'Captain Jack Holt,' the railroad savage, were 'Scar Faced Charley,' 'Shacknasty Jim,' 'Lonely Wolf,' 'Square-Nosed Ike,' 'Scalp Snatcher,' 'Lava-bed William,' 'Great Father's Son,' 'Washington Murphy,' 'Ulysses' Bull Dog,' 'Reporters' Skull Scraper,' 'Much Mush Johnny,' 'Starve-us-not-Phillip,' 'Let-us-have-wings Tommy,' and others with names equally as poetical and expressive. The savages were scattered through the streets to prevent the ladies from stealing the pigs. The big chiefs, however, rode in a gaily decorated wagon, with a 'News' reporter as interpreter.

THE KU-KLUX KLANS.

The K.K.K.'s, about whom so much has been said, and who caused so much legislation and stir in Washington, were telegraphed for, and assisted in safely escorting the pigs from South Broadway to the armory. They were in charge of D. W. Gillespy, who has been missing from the community since the close of the late onpleasantness. Their grim visages and mortuary costumes inspired an awe suitable to the occasion. The police, though armed with revolvers and clubs, stood aside and seemed to say, 'Mr. Ku-Kluxes, please pass on off my beat.' An old lady, who had stepped out to get a cent's worth of milk, and who doubtless had not read the 'News,' was taken by surprise at the approach of the savages, and caused some merriment by darting into the house, and spilling the lacteal fluid over her new Fourth of July dress. The last seen of her, she was hanging out of a third-story window with a broom in her hand, looking to see if any of the varmints had got loose from the gang and were lagging behind.

THE PIGS.

The pigs were mounted on a gaily festooned express wagon drawn by the finest horses in the city. During the route of procession, when they would recognize any of the boys of the Fifth who chanced to be undisguised, the porkers, who squealed from fright, seemed to know what the regiment did at Mr. Baker's farm while they were there, and trembled for their lives.

BABES IN THE WOOD.

Immediately behind the pigs, on the same wagon, lay the infant that was found in the woods by the Fifth during their fête at Ridge Hill Farms.

The devil kept an eye on old father Time, as the last-named gently brushed the flies from off the baby with a palm-leaf fan. Garbage horns were used to amuse the babe and keep it from crying.

THE ROUTE OF PROCESSION.

The route of procession was the same as printed in the

daily papers. Broadway was densely crowded by anxious
bystanders of all classes in life, who were eager to witness
the carnival. As the procession moved along Baltimore
Street, the crowd swelled at every step, and when it at
length halted at the armory, the multitude was countless.

AT THE ARMORY.

Upon reaching Parade Avenue, the lost baby, whom
some one thought was little Charlie Ross, was carried in
and laid upon the floor. It did some crying, as was naturally expected, the large hall being filled with strangers.
Some candies were administered, but the youngster continued to yell until some one spoke of sirup of squills and
paregoric, and then the infantile music at once ceased, and
the ladies took it in charge and put it in its little bed.

BRING ON YOUR PIGS.

The squeakers were next seized by the Modocs and carried in, guarded by the K.K.K.'s. A gun-stand was placed
in the centre of the spacious armory, and the objects of
attraction carefully laid upon it. The ladies in the
galleries tried the suicidal plan of letting themselves drop
from their elevated position in their anxiety to welcome
the little guests, but they were held back by their gentlemen friends. As 'Loney' is young and tender, a guard
was placed around him to keep off the rush. The officers

who had been mounted on mules sent them home to their owners. The crowd soon dispersed, and the grandest carnival that Baltimore ever witnessed was at an end."

The Hog — *Porcus* (or *Suidæ Sus* of the ancients) — family, in its wild and in its domesticated state, has habits which make it prominent above all other animals.

They are thick-skined, and to the general observer are obtuse in most of their faculties. To the contrary, however, their sense of smell, sight and taste are in high perfection. The sense of hearing is very acute. They prefer vegetable to animal food. They are voracious, bold, and of immense strength. In their wild state they are the fiercest denizens of the forests of Europe and Asia. The lower grade called *peccary*, found extensively in Central and South America, is of a small size, and although not so strong as the true hog, yet most disagreeable to contend with, and man has but a slight chance of escape if attacked by them. They herd together, and are said to have leaders, or such as direct them in their fights. If taken young, they display great affection for such as are kind to them, and affiliate with dogs or other pet animals.

There are many species of the hog family which are only of the Irish-cousin relationship or family to the perfected *porcus*, such as the *Guinea pig*, the *hog-deer* of Java and the Indian Archipelago, the four-horned hog of Abyssinia. The *water hog*, semi-web-footed, lives upon fruit, corn, sugar-canes, and eats all the fish it can catch. The Spanish *tatous* (hogs in armor), the Dutch *porcupine*, called the *iron-hog:* the *porpoise* has by some been designated as the *sea-hog*, and Aristotle writes of the *hog-ape*.

More than of any other animal, naturalists have studied the habits of the hog family.

Cuvier's memoir on the fossil bones of the hog, to the French Academy, in 1809, Professor Owen in his work on Brtish Fossil Mammalia, and numerous other writers, have attracted the attention of other than naturalists to this higher order of animal life.

The term hog is derived from a Hebrew word, meaning *to encompass* or *surround ;* suggested by the round figure in his fat and most natural state, and '' narrow eyes.''

1491 B.C., Moses inscribed those laws which imply that pork must have been the prevailing food of the Israelites prior to that date. The Greeks held it in high esteem, while with the Romans every art was put in practice to impart a finer and more delicate flavor to the flesh, to gratify the epicureanism of this people.

Pliny writes that they fed swine on dried figs, and drenched them to repletion with honeyed wine. The *Porcus Trojanus* was a very celebrated dish, and one that eventually became so extravagantly expensive, that a sumptuary law was passed respecting it. It consisted of a whole hog with the entrails drawn out, and the inside stuffed with thrushes, larks, becaficos, oysters, nightingales, and delicacies of every kind, and the whole bathed in wine and gravies. Another dish was a hog served whole, the one side roasted, the other boiled.

Varro records that the Gauls produced the finest swine's flesh, and Strabo reports that in the reign of Augustus, they supplied Rome and all Italy with gammons, hog-pudding, hams and sausages.*

Some of the ancients have held the hog as entitled to divine honor. In the Island of Crete it was regarded as sacred, and in several parts of India it was regarded as the favored of the gods, and the best intermediator for man. The Jews, Egyptians, and followers of Mohammed, alone appear to have abstained from its use. Tacitus writes that the Jews abstained from it in consequence of a leprosy to which the hog is very subject. Plutarch and other writers write concerning the flesh being strong, oleaginous, difficult of digestion, and liable to produce cutaneous diseases; and state that the Israelites were overrun with

---

* Two young graduates of Harvard College, resident in Southboro' and Framingham, Mass., are now doing the same work for our Boston, excepting only the hog pudding, which no doubt would have a large sale if as dainty as their sweetmeats of pork.

leprosy at the period of their quitting Egypt. Thus Moses found it necessary to enact a law prohibiting the use of swine flesh. Plutarch states that those who drank the milk of the swine, became blotchy and leprous.

Abstinence being necessary to health, the burning sun in Egypt, Syria, and parts of Greece, will account for the prohibition of pork by the priests and legislators.

" Order is Heaven's first law."   " Cleanliness is next to godliness." The hog is naturally much more cleanly in his habits than many of those who say he isn't.

A writer in the sixteenth century asserts squarely, that " the hog is the cleanest of all animals." Many other naturalists endorse this. Martin writes, that " if the stye or yard be covered with filth, it is as disgraceful to the keeper as it is injurious to the animal. The hog actually suffers, for naturally he delights in clean straw; his twinkling eyes and low grunt expressing his feelings of contentment." *

---

* The " Naturalist Library" gives this incident : " A pig that had been kept several days a close prisoner to his stye, was let out for the purpose of its being cleansed and his bed replenished. The pig immediately ran to the stable, from which he carried several sheaves of straw to his stye, each time holding them in his mouth by the band. The straw, being intended for another use, was carried back to the stable; but the pig, at the first favorable opportunity, regained it."

The only motive which induces the hog to wallow in the mire is to protect his skin in the heat of summer from the scorching rays of the sun, and from the attack of winged-insect persecutors. In France, the traveller will find the pig in the houses of the peasantry, scrupulously neat, and displaying great affection towards those who are kind to them. This bond of sympathy becomes so strong that when the killing-time comes, the services of a neighbor have to be asked to kill their *pet.*

The pig, if allowed his liberty, will avoid all filth, and if petted will become as obedient as the dog, and display a greater sagacity or reasoning power. Darwin says, "It is a sure sign of cold wind when pigs collect straw in their mouths and run about crying loudly." Foster says, "When hogs shake the stalks of corn, and thereby spoil them. it indicates rain." Linnæus records that "the hog is more nice in the selection of his vegetable diet than any of our other domesticated herbivorous animals, rejecting all but 72 varieties of plants, while the horse, sheep, goat and cow eat from 262 to 449 varieties.

In France and Italy, swine are employed in hunting for truffles, that grow six inches below the surface of the soil; wherever they stop and begin to root with their nose, truffles will invariably be found. If, then, as naturalists assert, the pig is gifted with an exquisite sense of smell, they must be acutely sensitive to all the injurious physical influences arising from the filth in which they are imprisoned, and their flesh must consequently be affected by trichinæa, or otherwise poisoned for table use. We are led to enlarge upon this subject of the *porcus* family, its care, &c., inasmuch as its flesh is more generally used for table food than that of any other animal.

It is the flesh food most preferred and consumed in each one of our union of States. By reference to the Statistical Department at Washington, we find that that portion of these which have been raised in the cornfields of the West are sound and healthy. But excepting a few, who care for their pigs as daintily as the Harvard graduates hereinbefore cited — who will no doubt be surprised at this unannounced allusion — most of the pigs raised among what may be called our home farmers, are kept in filthy pens and yards, and the flesh is unfit for market.

The flesh of those swine fed on city garbage is liable to be unfit for market, inasmuch as this garbage is often fermented and sour. And thus the City of Boston, by the disposition of its garbage, directly aids — unless by a more thorough supervision by its Board of Health — in filling our hospital wards with patients diseased from eating unwholesome pork.

And here may be the proper place to inform you that we have led you, reader, purposely in the dark as to the REAL object of this printed *Guide*. We have apparently digressed from our guide-walk, and introduced history, mythology, and alluded to peculiar acts of city officials; but there has been a motive in all this — partly to interest and amuse, but looking toward a reform much needed in this age so tinctured with bribery and legislative or other executive enactments to benefit the few at the expense of the many. Will you co-operate in this reform? Please to take out your pencil and jot down your approval or criticisms upon this that herein follows.

Agassiz tells us that fish diet improves the brain. Although the fish has the smallest brain, compared to its size, of all animal life, Agassiz's statement may possibly be true, by reason of the phosphates composing its flesh; yet he omits to inform us that the cookery of fish lets go the phosphates or ozmozone, consequently the brain would be much more active if we did, as consumers of their own species do, swallow the fish alive, and thus get *all* the phosphates.*

* The recent discoveries of a gentleman in the State of Maine, that the juices expressed from the flesh of the manhaden, separated from the oil, is not distinguishable, when similarly served, from beef tea, is destined to revolutionize our hospital life, and, we hope, will

If fish diet improve the brain of the human species, may
we not adduce the fact that swine flesh will debase or ele-
vate the intellect of our race, according as it is more or less
inflicted by trichinæa, from being imprisoned in filthy
pens and yards?

Although the writer never eats any part of the swine,
he yet believes its flesh may agree, when properly bred
and cured, with others' palates.

The Hog family displays more intellect, or are intuitively more susceptible of education, than any other animal.
In recognition of this we have the " Porcellian Club," one
of the most reclusive of the social clubs at the Harvard
University. There was on exhibition in Philadelphia,
during the Centennial season, an educated pig, of which
many have been exhibited throughout the country. By
kind treatment he has been taught to look at your
watch, and on being asked to tell you the time, to
pick up and deposit at your feet the number or numbers nearest to the hour indicated by your watch.
On being asked to tell you who was one of the
greatest statesmen of our age, or in answer to other questions worded by the visitor, he would pick up the card

lessen the quantity of poisoned leaf tea now imported from the so-
called " heathen Chinee," who seems to be, however, " civilized" in
his adulterations.

having the name of Daniel Webster, or of some other, upon it as would in piggy's mind (?) properly answer the question. Arithmetical questions in addition, multiplication and subtraction were also correctly answered. This was by no trick of the showman. Similarly educated pigs are recorded by naturalists. One was exhibited in Pall Mall, London, in the year 1789, which had been taught to pick up letters, written upon pieces of card, and arrange them into words. As the Universal Yankee Nation are known as a "*calculating*" race, it is eminently proper that this animal of mind, the calculating Hog, should symbolize us as a nation.

We have no cause then to be ashamed of the porcineograph designed by the host at Ridge Hill Farms, and given by him as a Centennial souvenir in 1876 to such residents in Virginia, South Carolina, and the South, as participated the previous year at the laying of the corner-stone of the Ridge Hill Farms Piggery.

It portrays the geographical outline of this Union of 38 States, exactly as shown by the U. S. surveys of 1870, to which, however, is added one imaginary leg with its foot resting on Cuba. It adopts Lower California as a second leg, and the third is shown reaching to Sandwich, pacifically the Sandwich Islands. Alas-*queue* is shown as the "caudal appendage" by special act of Congress; and it only requires the angle of Canadian territory between the Northern Lakes, called *Hydro-Cephalus*, because it is the "Reciprocity Passage," to complete the gehography of the United States.

The corner-stone of the Piggery was laid with all due formality, the voluntary offerings from the guests placed thereunder, consisting of buttons cut from the military coats, coins, and all sorts of keepsakes from the pocket, pipes of peace, newspapers from Boston, Rhode Island, New York, Virginia, North and South Carolina, and other States, &c., &c.

One of the Boston newspapers, when giving an account of this fête, reported that there was a great demand for souvenirs, and that "three Governors were seen hanging to one rope" when lowering the corner-stone to its place. This was only two thirds true, inasmuch as the Governors of Massachusetts and Rhode Island were active in this duty; but Colonel Andrews, who was sent to represent the State as spokesman, was not the Governor of South Carolina, although he soon would be if the election rested with the Boston ladies.

Leaving the Corner-stone Piggery, the visitor will turn south by the borders of Charles River, then east up Bellevue Avenue to and either by Pine Avenue through the pine woods on Charity Hill, to the open field east of

the Windmill Tower, or else continue on Bellevue Avenue,
on hill, through dale and pine groves skirting the ser-
.pentine Charles River, for one mile, to the house now in
course of alteration, commenced September 1st, for
summer boarders in 1878. This house stands on high
land, which shelves down to the Riverside Plateau, like
an inverted bowl, reminding the traveller of the castel-
lated hills on the River Rhine.

This (unless some better name is selected) may be
called the *Governors' Castle,* inasmuch as it may be used
to shelter such of the Governors of our respective States
as accept hospitalities in these quarters, and participate in
laying the corner-stone of the Ridge Hill Laboratory.

The first step toward the erection of this Laboratory on
the Pine Ridge, southeast of the Windmill Tower, was
taken on August 27, 1877, by Mr. Greaves setting the first
levelling stake, and Eddie, the elder son of the proprietor,
removing the first shovelful of earth. On September 3, at
six o'clock P.M., Master Eddie Farnsworth Baker, with
his six-year-old brother, Walter Farnsworth Baker, laid
and cemented the first stone of the foundation for the
corner-stone at the northeast corner, as has been the
custom from remote ages. Kernels of corn and crumbs
of bread, emblems of food staples, were strewn upon the
cement by the thirteen guests assembled, who sang "Amer-

ica," " When shall we meet again," and other appropriate hymns, and the improvised ceremonies ended.

Adjacent to this Laboratory there has been commenced, September 1, the digging for the foundation of a building to be erected under the management of Mr. Alfred Green, builder, of Philadelphia, to be completed this fall, with over one hundred dormitories for the accommodation of summer boarders in 1878. Unless a better name is suggested, this will be known as the HOTEL TREPHIS, from the Greek word *trepho*, meaning to nourish. It will be under the management of such employés of the Massachusetts Institute of Cookery, which is to have its headquarters in Boston. whose services are not required in Boston during the warm months of summer.

The Philadelphia Fairmount Park Commissioners ordered all the Centennial buildings removed from the Park grounds, and consequently these buildings were bought at auction, at such a sacrifice that this will cost, when finished, at Ridge Hill Farms, discarding all but the frame timbers and ornamental work, and using new stock for outside and inside finishing. only one third of that which it originally cost at Philadelphia.

The Restaurant and Café connected with the Ridge Hill Hotel will cater to the wants of the two or three thousand of visitors now weekly visiting the Ridge Hill Farms, and of such clubs or special parties as wish to pass one day or more in the *Tharis* Home Hotel, in the pine woods, and in boating and fishing on Charles River.

The initiatory step has been taken toward this Restaurant; and in order to get familiar somewhat with the capacity of those soliciting positions as teachers in the Institute of Cookery, there has been established a Lunch Department connected with the Registry Office, where visitors can obtain a cold lunch, or, by prior order given at 13 West Street, Boston, or at the Registry Office, can get a specially prepared hot dinner served in one of the rooms of the Virginia Lodge, which is adjacent to the Registry Office.

Preliminary to the organization of the Massachusetts Institute of Cookery, there will be opened in November, under the direction of the projectors of this work, a School of Cookery at 158 Tremont Street, Boston. Early application should be made at 13 West Street by those desiring to join the classes, which will be composed of from six to twelve, and must at the outset be limited in number.

In addition to teaching the art of Sanitary Cookery, there will be classes in the use of the microscope for the detection of adulterations of articles used for table food, for the study of the condition or purity and wholesomeness of animal food, and the study of the elements producing fungi, or decomposing their material or the air which supplies the breath of life, with kindred subjects, in November next, at the Boston Aquarium, 13 West Street, Boston.

This is that which has been too long neglected, and dependent upon which is the health and intelligence of our race. Should we not regard cause and effect as studiously as Moses regarded the sanitary state of his people, and as the Romans by enacting sumptuary laws controlled their race from degeneracy? Is it not true that the brain is acutely sensitive to that with which the stomach is fed? Of what use are our higher universities of learning, if we neglect the so-called cook, whose lack of knowledge of sanitary cookery so upsets physically as to render the brain *dormant* to all tuition, no matter how learned the teacher? If the National and State Executive encourage institutions for the education of our race, is it not of equal — yea, of prior and fundamental — importance that it should seek to control the brain towards educational influences, by enacting laws, and the appointment of special officers to enforce the same, CONTROLLING —

First, the breeding and care of animals whose flesh is intended for consumption;

Second, the adulterations of articles intended for table or animal food;*

* Through inefficient laws, or the inefficient enforcement of the laws, this may be truthfully known as *The Adulterated Age*, inasmuch as purity is rare, and adulteration abundant.

Third, by encouraging with a fostering care such institutions as shall teach the art of *preparing* articles intended for consumption, and that of SANITARY COOKERY, which, more than other science, controls the intelligence of our race.

Is it presuming too much to hope that our Civil-service President, and his Temperance Reform help-mate, may find it both agreeable, convenient, and think it their official duty, to aid or encourage the establishment of such co-operative *Institutes of Cookery*, in each one of our thirty-eight United States?

The *prevention* of disease among our general citizens of all classes, as well as in the army corps, is of more consequence than attention to its *cure* by the Medical Department. Then is it not of such paramount importance as to justify the executive thought to the cause and effect of this that may save the intellect of our entire race; that elevates or debases and intoxicates the Executive, Legislature and Judiciary, and is the foundation of crime, degeneracy and its attendant pandemonium? Would that the heads of the National Executive could regard this movement with such interest as to determine to accommodate other duties to the endorsement by their presence at the start of this new movement, namely, the laying of the corner-stone of the Laboratory on the Charity Reserva-

tion at Ridge Hill Farms, which (with the Governors'
Castle) is to be under the management of the organization we wish to establish, with headquarters in Boston,
under the name of "THE MASSACHUSETTS INSTITUTE OF
COOKERY." We hope that the Governors, those executive heads of the several States, who may at this Fête
assemble, will take such active interest in this important
work as to encourage the establishing of sister or co-associate institutes for cookery in their respective States.

Cannot those Executive officials of each of our Union
of States, accommodate their duties at home to their
attendance at the Fête day, September 20th, 1877; reaching the estate on September 19th, and there remaining
after the Fête in social re-union for the benefit of con-
currence in other matters of social science until Monday,
September 24th? *Should* any of the National Executive
department at Washington favorably consider this urgent
hope for their presence, there will be placed at their
disposal the only "White House" on the estate, while
the State Executives will have quarters in the Governors' Castle, the Virginia Lodge and the Singed-Cat
Cottage (an old Centennial farm mansion, so called because more comfortable inside than the outer shell indicates).

May we expect the sympathy of the State Legislature

in granting such pecuniary or other concessions as shall develop the grains of seed into the full-grown plant?

May we not hope that the officials of the city of Boston will regard this work as of equal importance to that of *free* travel on the East Boston ferries?

Is it asking too much of the City of Boston that its school committee require the study, by the senior female class in all our public schools, of that medical chemistry that is the foundation of our physical system, that prevents or causes disease, that dormatizes or increases the vigor of the brain,—in fact, upon which depends the intelligence of our race? We mean that chemical knowledge of the composition of every article used in the preparation of table food, and the chemical product of assimilating any two or more of them. Is the education of the female complete without a knowledge of these chemicals which are the make-up of hygienic cookery? Is not cookery the basis of vigorous health of both body and mind, according as those who cater to our food requirements supply us with that which is composed of *un*adulterated materials of the best quality, so assimilated by heat as to retain the ozone or electric air, helping solution with animal juices of the animal flesh, and be made palatable by an attractive aroma, or of disease, imbecility and death, by our recklessly bolting that pandemonium of vegetable and animal oil and grease, in solution, with nitric, sulphuric and muriatic acids, a combination of mineral and chemical poisons which incites a taste for those fluids which completes the work and embalms the physical and enfeebles the mental organs of those who crowd our streets, our executives, our hospitals, and finally our beautiful cemeteries?

The intelligence of our race is, without doubt, more distributed; but are the *literati* of the so-called " Modern Athens," Boston, in advance of that of the old savans in ancient Greece?

Do we give that attention to sumptuary laws, to the annihilation of all offenders who manufacture or sell poison adulterated with our food materials? Are the cunning arts and devices of such offenders sufficiently subject to the criminal courts?

Are the people properly protected by the Judiciary from these poisonous influences which sap the foundation of all sanitary laws, destroy health, induce crime, and tend generally to the demoralization of hygienics, as well as to law and order?

Do not the cunning arts of the advocate, procrastinate the trial, and then by some legal quibble, make inoperative the punishment for offences notoriously proved?

Do we not need new measures to conform with the *peculiar* CUNNING of the age—a judiciary of *public opinion* which shall not be trammelled by town or State lines, but whose decisions against offenders of our social life, be it from poisoning our food from selfish gain, or by attacks on individual character in the public prints, or by other encroachments on individual rights and social exclusiveness?

Can we get justice in a more sure, prompt and efficient fashion through the courts, or by the establishment of such a conservative board of honorable men, above reproach and political bias, for each ward, district, State, and the nation, each in affiliation with the other, as shall calmly hear all evidence, *pro* and *con.*, decide the guilt or innocence, and the punishment of the guilty by such a re-establishment of the old-fashioned *pillory* as shall monumentalize the acts of the offender to the odium of the general public?

Reader, do you sympathize with this thought? Will you join the " FRIDAY SOCIAL REFORM CLUB," devoted to denouncing, in such fashion as may be best for the general good, for general ODIUM in the pillory, located in public resorts in the city and State, on every Friday (hangman's day) such offences as shall be decided as worthy of desecration, by a Conservative Executive?

Will not those in each ward or subdivision of ward, town or city, who sympathize with this plan select a few energetic men, of reliable reputation, to act as lieutenants,

captains, supervisors and conservative counsellors, and push
hard to organize a subdivision of the Friday Reform Club? *

* At the time of the Boston fire of November 10, 1872, a trader on
Winter Street, Boston, had verbally agreed to lease an estate to one who
had made every preparation to occupy it; but the contract not having
been signed on Monday, November 11, the lessor sends word to the con-
tracting party that he must agree to pay five hundred dollars per annum
additional, or he should refuse to sign the lease; to which dishonorable
extortion he was compelled to yield, having gone too far to recede without a greater expense.

At the time of the Globe Theatre district fire, May 30, 1873, the father
of this extortioner was guilty of exactly the same act; in this case the
owner of Ridge Hill Farms was the sufferer, and 13 West Street the
subject matter.   More recently this same man, learning that the lease of
one who had occupied the same warehouse for many years would soon
terminate, and that the occupant would be greatly inconvenienced if
compelled to move, by connivance contracted with the lessor at an ad-
vanced rent, and turning on the occupant, compelled him to pay him
fifteen hundred dollars bonus for the renewed lease.

The judiciary does not reach such cases. A court of public opinion,
only, can tend to prevent a repetition of such offences against honorable
dealing.

If such as sympathize with such an organization, will *evidence* their
interest, by getting their friends, acquaintances and neighbors to notify
their *desire* to join, and also to subscribe for, say " The Friday Record
and Social Science Weekly," a small-sized newspaper, devoted, 1st,
to sanitary cookery, new preparations, best methods of making bread,
preservation of articles intended for table food, best modes of trans-
porting animal food, detection of adulterations in articles intended for
table food, &c.;

2d. Friday Pillory or Correctionary Department. Examination of
offences by individual, public press, &c., against personal rights; epi-

The organization of the Massachusetts Institute of Cookery, as projected by the proprietor of Ridge Hill Farms, is as follows, but which may be materially amended by the sober reflections of those co-associating to work out the scheme : —

1st. Organization as a corporation under the general

taphs, caricatures and illustrations, monumentalizing such as are offenders against the laws of society, making the editor or proprietor responsible for errors of his apprentice who has been allowed the columns of the respectable journal " to sling malicious ink; "

3d. To similarly epitaphilize such officials as yield to the peculiar pressure of interested parties, and so legislate for the benefit of the few as shall be at the expense of the many.

The first care of this order to be that of taking every possible step to prevent thirty-nine fortieths of the capital represented in Boston proper, from paying the cost of running the FREE ferriage for the one fortieth represented by residents in East Boston *im*proper; and also devoting our heads, hands, feet and pocket-books in preventing the re-election of such officials as voted for, and do not now recant, this precedent, so dishonorable and damaging to the best interests of the City of Boston.

Members of this *Friday Club* should not be bound to vote for any one to political office, merely because such or such an one was a member of "our club." Many deliberate villains join churches, and to the world are very devout, but are finally found to be wolves in sheep's clothing; and every caution should be taken to prevent political bias warping the executive of this Friday Club.

Therefore each member should have entire liberty of conscience to act and vote as he pleases. But when there is no appearance of guile, it is supposed the members will all vote as the executive may, after a sober hearing of all sides, decide as proper.

statutes, or, as will doubtless be preferred, under a special charter from, and with perhaps some pecuniary assistance of the State Legislature.

2d. Shares one hundred dollars each. Capital varying from one hundred thousand to one million dollars, depending upon the erection of a building for the Boston headquarters, and upon the practical sympathy given to this work by capitalists, who invest from their hope of good dividends, and from the benevolent, who subscribe for shares in their *own* and that of others' names, whom they wish to compliment, as *trustees*, for the benefit of THE MASSACHUSETTS TREPHO-PHAGIAN INSTITUTE (from the Greek *trephein*, to nourish, *phagien*, to eat), which is strictly a charity, to distribute delicacies of sanitary cookery, &c., to the invalid poor. This food-dispensary institute getting all its supplies from the Institute of Cookery, and paying for them with the dividends on its funds invested in the capital stock of this Institute of Cookery.

In furtherance of this plan, the owner of Ridge Hill Farms proposes to deed the so-called Charity Reservation of his estate, comprising three hundred and fifty acres of land every way suitable for agricultural purposes, as well as having all the *desiderata* of pine woods, boating, fishing, &c., required by summer recreationists, to the *Trepho-Phagian Institute*, to form one part, at such sum as may be decided, of its stock in the capital of the Institute of Cookery. The building and work now just commenced, he proposes shall be at the cost of the Institute that receives them.

This large and valuable territory already has two large barns, capable of sheltering over one hundred cows, besides other buildings, including the Corner-stone Piggery, &c.

The National Government has made reservations of funds from the sale of Government lands, in aid of agricultural colleges teaching the art of production of food supplies. Are such institutes of cookery as teach how to prepare these food supplies, as shall best control the intelligence and the *physique* of our race, unworthy of similar aid and encouragement?

The Commonwealth of Massachusetts has made appropriation in aid of the Agassiz School of Zoology, at Harvard University, amounting to three hundred and twenty-three thousand dollars.

It has aided in publishing Harris' great work on "Insects Injurious to Vegetation." It has given a fostering care to the food supplies cultivated in our rivers and on our coasts, by the appointment and payment of fish commissioners.

It should now pass one general act requiring all towns

and cities to stock with fish, in order to purify the waters of the same, such ponds, lakes or streams whence they obtain their water supplies. Will it not commence by requiring Brookline and Newton to stock with fish the waters of Charles River, inasmuch as fish are regarded as the most efficient purifiers?

The Commonwealth should encourage its State Board of Health to investigate minutely and enforce all laws relating to the adulterations of articles offered for sale for table food. And may not the Commonwealth, with equal propriety, make an appropriation in aid of this Massachusetts Institute of Cookery?

The several towns and cities of this Commonwealth are permitted, and do make investments in railroads and other works of public improvement: may not this Massachusetts Institute of Cookery be regarded as a public improvement very much needed, and one pointing to the good of all?

The City of Boston has expended between one and two millions of dollars for the Danvers Insane Hospital; and millions for its City Hospital, court-houses, jails, and other correctionary institutions.

It has annually appropriated about five thousand dollars for the *free* distribution of soup, from the police stations, to the famished, suffering from the stagnation in commerce and manufactures.

Then may it not, with economy to its treasury, appropriate one hundred or two hundred thousand dollars towards the erection of an edifice in Boston for use as the headquarters of the Massachusetts Institute of Cookery, wherein all the female members of the senior classes in our public schools may be educated in that art of chemical and of sanitary cookery, which, more than any other science, is the basis of intelligence or depravity of our age, and to a large extent the prevention of that disease and crime which compels the erection of hospitals, court-houses and jails?

If the City of Boston is to feed its famishing, it can be better done by giving coupons for deliveries of soup at the branch stations of the Cookery Institute, where that prepared by superior experts can be had at as low a cost as that produced in the police stations, where the deserving poor naturally are averse to go for it. By so doing, there is no scorching of the *amour propre*, inasmuch as the charity coupon may not be discernible from that bought by those more favored with this world's pecuniary comforts.

These branch selling depots will serve a large class who will not steal, cannot beg, and at present prices, particularly in Boston, where flesh food is higher than in New York, Philadelphia or Baltimore, are restricted from buying. This institution can buy at wholesale at less than one half that paid by the consumer, and can save fully another twenty-five per cent (in all say three fourths), by utilizing the residuum, and methodizing work, and expenditures on the factory system. This institution, by its branch salesrooms, will enable many to be independent of those social grievances, the house servant, which now migrate from A to B, and from B to A, because their mutations increase the fees of, and therefore are not frowned upon by, the proprietor of that well-known institution, very properly called the "Intelligence" Office, as it certainly does control the "intelligence" of our race more than the Boston schools or Harvard University.

The City of Boston is most certainly warranted in encouraging the work here outlined, by a liberal appropriation, or by investment in its capital, as cities invest in other works of public improvement. The Boston City Board of Health should work with it and be of it. The poison imported in tea should be exposed, and dealers punished. The students, male and female, in our public schools, should be taught chemical analysis, and the use of the microscope, and how to detect the adulterations in sugar, pepper, coffee, flour, and nearly three out of four of our food staples, which are now undermining the vigor or physique of our age.

The Board of Health can affiliate in many ways with such an institution. It may study if it be practicable to control the mixing of water and milk, which tends to fearfully increase the mortality list of infants, by laws compelling producers of milk to send it to market in receptacles holding not over two quarts, with a slip of paper pasted from can neck over the stopper, showing by its being torn or broken, that some one has tampered with the milk. This paper, having the name of the producer printed upon it, will make him responsible for brewers' grain or Indian meal milk, and give him a reputation accordingly. The Board of Health, in common with this Institute of Cookery, should print monthly, and when necessary, weekly, a circular-sized newspaper, offered to subscribers at not over one dollar the year, containing reports of analyses of adulterations, a *pillory* column of those detected in adulterations, sanitary laws, recommendations for the comfort of the healthy as well as of the invalid, how to protect man and beast from mosquito trials of life, and to be used as a communicator with the Boards of Health of other cities, and as an authoritative advertiser of those sanitary grievances which should be copied in the public journals in all sections of our country.

The City of Boston is most certainly warranted in encouraging this work by a liberal appropriation. Will it be done by the city officials of the present year?

All such as take any interest in these matters, may notify their wish to subscribe for stock in the capital of the Massachusetts Institute of Cookery, in their own behalf, or as trustee for the Food Dispensary, by notifying any of the following Trepho-Phagian committee : —

HARVEY D. PARKER,	EDWIN CHAPIN,
MRS. S. T. HOOPER,	MRS. JAMES BROWNE,
MRS. OLIVER DITSON,	MRS. OSBORNE HOWES.

TRUSTEES.

Ex-Gov. WM. GASTON,	CHARLES M. CLAPP,
J. W. CANDLER,	ISAAC FENNO,
Dr. JOSEPH BURNETT,	WM. E. BAKER,
JEROME JONES,	EDW'D FARNSWORTH BAKER,

WALTER FARNSWORTH BAKER :

or by calling and subscribing at 13 West Street, Boston.

This committee will also have supervision of and decision as to awarding ten prizes to such as shall send to 13 West Street, Boston, in time to be practically tested at the Governors' Fête on September 20, at the laying of the corner-stone of the Institute Laboratory at Ridge Hill Farms, the best samples of bread made by the sender, or of some approved new dish of cookery, best recipe for preparing any special kind of cookery, &c. All bread should be sent well packed from dampness.

All such as wish to subscribe any large or small sum toward a permanent fund for the Trepho-Phagian Institute may notify any of the above-named committee.

Such as believe that trying is succeeding, and that it is our duty to ACT, and not listlessly remain passive, thinking we cannot change or get out of old ruts, those who sympathize with this suggested FRIDAY REFORM CLUB, should select some men above reproach or political bias in their respective wards, districts, towns, cities or counties, as Quartermasters, Lieutenants, Captains, Colonels of the Grand Friday Reform Army, and such as shall compose a conse ative Board of Counsellors, and push this work till you also stir up and incite an active interest in this work by receiving numerous letters from you, the following gentlemen, who, however, will know of this project for the first time on reading it in this book, but whom we desire to interest as principals in this work, and hope to do so, if you, reader, that sympathize with the plan, will only write them, signifying your wish to join, and thus incite them to take hold: Ex-Governor William Gaston, Ex-Mayor Otis Norcross, Ex-Mayor Frederic W. Lincoln, Henry P. Kidder, Henry Lee, Marshall P. Wilder, Joseph Burnett, Harvey D. Parker, R. C. Greenleaf, Albert Bowker, Nathaniel J. Bradlee, Samuel Johnson, Thomas Gaffield. Our interest in the work must be our apology for thus using these names without the knowledge of any one of them, and thus, of course, in no way making them responsible for this our assumptive act. Pleading guilty to bringing these conservative modest men into print, and of skirting the edge of the globe in our social-science rambles, if we have bored you with this long epistle you have yourself to blame for reading the effusions of your friend, who wishes both to amuse and interest you in a good work.

CRAYONATED SCIENCE.

INDEX GUIDE.

References may be made to the map, but please make allowance for the numbers thereon differing from the numbers herein.

	PAGE
1. Permission to visit Ridge Hill Farms . .	3
2. Register your name at Registry Office . .	4
3. Visit Norino Tower, Arcadium, Tivoli Hall	6, 7, 8
4. Black and Gold Stable	5, 8
5. Coons in Pavilion Grove	11
6. Album Bowling Alley	9
7. Diorama, green wood-work, wire sides . .	12
8. African Porcupine in oval enclosure . .	12
9. Cages containing Cockatoos, Parrots, Macaws	12
10. Squirrel Cages	11
11. Leaky-Boot Fountain	11
12. Pavilion	11
13. Cage of Ring-neck Doves	11, 12
14. Mushroom Seats	24
15. Pass through Minnehaha's Wigwam . .	24
16. Eddie's and Walter's Gardens, and their Play and Ware House	24

		PAGE
17.	Goat enclosure	15, 16
18.	Balustrade Walk to Chapel	25
19.	Chapel	9
20.	Floral Avenue	26
21.	Monkey Building	13
22.	Conservatory of new Hot-houses	26
23.	Pass to the South of the owner's residence	26, 67
24.	Mosaic Gardens	28
25.	Camp John Adams	33
26.	Union Monument	33
27.	Chilian Pavilion	44
28.	Octagon Bear-Pit — Seneca Bears	17, 21, 44
29.	Gnome Drinking Fountain	44
30.	Arboretum Walks, Basin Spring Fountain	45
31.	Arboretum Lodge	46
32.	Boat-house	47
33.	Frog Fountain	46
34.	Coliseum Bridge	46
35.	Rustic Bridge	46, 50, 51
36.	Circular Bear-Pit	51
37.	Steamboat Landing	51
38.	Peacock House	52
39.	Deer Park, Buffaloes, Bison, Elk	52
40.	Krino Valley, right side	55

		PAGE
41.	Krino Valley, left side	61
42.	Rustic Seat and Umbrella	61
43.	Gothic Arch and Smugglers' Cove	61
44.	Entrance to Crystal Tower	62
45.	Smugglers' Cave	63
46.	Flirtation Tunnel	63
47.	Stalactite Grotto	63
48.	Turnstile	65
49.	Boston Fire Monument	52
50.	Circular Bear-Pit	65
51.	Camera Obscura	65
52.	Photograph Studio	66
53.	Registry Office	4, 66, 68
54.	Charity Reservation	29, 111
55.	Windmill Tower	29
56.	Riverside Herd Barn	111
57.	Corner-Stone Piggery	113, 132
58.	Governors' Castle	133
59.	Ridge Hill Laboratory (for the Mass. Institute of Cookery, headquarters in Boston), and the Trephis Home Hotel for summer boarders	134, 144

MISCELLANEOUS.

| 60. | Ladies' Cottage | 44 |
| 61. | Gentlemen's Cottage, rear of Bowling Alley | |

PAGE

62. Gentlemen's Walk 44

63. Friday Reform Club 89, 140, 151

64. Trepho-Phagian Institute . . . 144, 150

65. Boston Aquarium, 13 West St.. Boston.

66. References to Executive Board of Boston free-
    ing the East Boston Ferries . 20, 88. 139, 143

67. Ridge Hill Farms Lunch Department . . 134

68. Porcus Family habits, litter-ary inclinations,
    &c. 123–31

69. Florida, Brevard County Wonders . . 19

70. Subscriptions to the Institute of Cookery 135. 143, 150
    Those subscribing ten shares in trust for
    Trepho-Phagian Institute, to be Patrons
    of this Food Dispensary. Those subscrib-
    ing four thousand dollars to be classed as
    Founders — all Stockholders to be invited
    guests at the 20th September Fête.

THE BOSTON AQUARIUM, 13 West Street, Boston, is established specially in aid of and is to be donated to the Trepho-Phagian Institute, and in the hope that it may result in inciting such an interest as will lead to an extensive Aquarium in Boston, for the education and amusement of the masses.

It has salt and fresh water departments, stocked with Seals, Beavers, Sea Robins, Anemones, Crabs, Lobsters, Trout, Salmon, and thousands of curious mammalia and crustacæa, the study of whose habits is both instructive and amusing.

IF you would keep
Your lips from slips
  Five things
Observe with care:
Of whom you speak,
To whom you speak,
  And how,
  And when,
  And where.

www.ingramcontent.com/pod-product-compliance
Lightning Source LLC
Chambersburg PA
CBHW020548270326
41927CB00006B/765